Contents

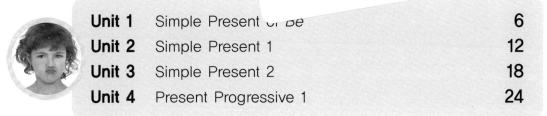

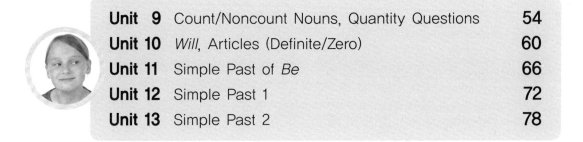

You are my

Grammar &

Speaking

1
Workbook

iam books

You are my
Grammar &
Speaking ①

Published by

I am Books

#1116, Daeryung Techno Town 12ᵗʰ Bldg.,

14, Gasan digital 2-ro, Geumcheon-gu, Seoul 153-778, Republic of Korea

TEL: 82-2-6343-0999

FAX: 82-2-6343-0995

Visit our website: http://www.iambooks.co.kr

Publishers: Shin Sunghyun, Oh Sangwook

Author: Lucifer EX

Editor: Kim Hyeona

Photo Credits:

Wikipedia (www.wikipedia.org): p. 18 (Jay-Z) ⓒ Joella Marano; p. 66 (Marilyn Monroe); p. 66 (Angelina Jolie) ⓒ Gage Skidmore; p. 67 (Yuri Gagarin); p. 67 (Leonardo da Vinci); p. 68 (Andre Kim) ⓒ Kinocine; p. 69 (Mozart; Van Gogh; Cleopatra; Alexander Graham Bell; Elvis Presley; Princess Grace; Diana, Princess of Wales); p. 69 (Bruce Lee) ⓒ Johnson Lau; p. 80 (Alexander Graham Bell); p. 120 (Mozart)

Flickr (www.flickr.com): p. 115 (Please Don't Pick the Flowers) ⓒ woofiegrrl

All other photos ⓒ imagetoday (www.imagetoday.co.kr)

ISBN: 978-89-6398-092-8 63740

After Finishing the Workbook

Book 1

Teacher's Comments

Parents' Comments

Class

Name

Unit 1 Simple Present of *Be*

Learn & Practice

Affirmatives

Subject + *Be* + Noun	Subject + *Be* + Adjective
She **is** an actress. We **are** doctors.	Tom **is** angry. They **are** tired.

- be 동사는 우리말 '~이다'의 뜻으로 주어에 따라 am, is, are 이렇게 세 가지가 있어요. 'be 동사 + 형용사'는 주어의
  상태 및 성질을 보충 설명해 주는 역할을 합니다.

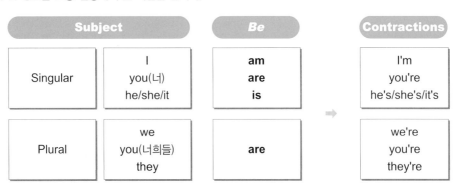

Subject		Be	Contractions
Singular	I you(너) he/she/it	am are is	I'm you're he's/she's/it's
Plural	we you(너희들) they	are	we're you're they're

Ⓐ Write the correct forms of *be* (*am, are, is*). Then write the short forms.

1. He ___is___ a bus driver. → ___He's___ a bus driver.

2. It _____ a smartphone. → _____ a smartphone.

3. You _____ a middle school student. → _____ a middle school student.

4. They _____ expensive. → _____ expensive.

5. She _____ a lawyer. → _____ a lawyer.

6. I _____ very happy. → _____ very happy.

Learn & Practice 2

Negative of *Be*: *Be* + *Not*

She **is not** a doctor.
(= She's not... / She isn't...)

We **are not** American.
(= We're not... / We aren't...)

They **are not** oranges.
(They're not... / They aren't...)

- be 동사 바로 뒤에 'not'만 붙이면 부정문이 돼요. 우리말로 '~이 아니다'라는 뜻으로 해석합니다. 축약형을 더 자주 쓰지만 am not을 줄여 amn't로 줄여 쓰진 않아요.

Contractions

I**'m not**	I amn't (X)
you**'re not**	you **aren't**
he/she/it**'s not**	he/she/it **isn't**
we/they**'re not**	we/they **aren't**

A Read and write as in the example. Use contractions.

1. China __isn't__ a city. It __is__ a country.
2. I ________ Spanish. I ________ Italian.
3. He ________ from Thailand. He ________ from Korea.
4. The questions ________ difficult. They ________ easy.
5. Michael and I ________ singers. We ________ dancers.

Learn & Practice 3

The Verb *Be*: *Yes/No* Questions

- be 동사의 의문문은 be 동사를 문장 맨 앞으로 보내고 물음표(?)를 써 주면 돼요. '~이니?, ~이 있니?'라고 물어보는 말이 됩니다.
- 대답은 be 동사를 그대로 사용하여 yes나 no로 대답하고, 주어는 알맞은 대명사로 바꾸어 대답해요. 부정의 대답은 축약하지만 긍정의 대답은 축약형을 쓰지 않아요.

Am	I	...?
Is	he/she/it	
Are	you/we/they	

Are you a thief?

Yes, **I am**.
No, **I'm not**.

A Make *yes/no* questions and answers.

1. She is a pianist.   Q: _____Is she a pianist?_____   A: No, ___she isn't___ .

2. It is a fork.   Q: _____   A: Yes, _____ .

3. The sun is a ball of fire. Q: _____   A: Yes, _____ .

4. They are vegetables.   Q: _____   A: No, _____ .

5. You are English teachers. Q: _____   A: No, _____ .

Statements with *There + Be*

There are two women and a man in this picture.
There is a coffee cup on the table.

Q: **Is there** a laptop on the table?
A: Yes, **there is**.

- there be는 우리말 '~가 있다'의 뜻으로 '존재'를 나타내요. be 동사 뒤에 나오는 명사가 주어이며 주어의 단수, 복수에 따라 is 또는 are를 쓸지가 결정돼요. 부정문은 be 동사와 마찬가지로 be 동사 바로 뒤에 not을 써요.
- 의문문은 be 동사를 문장 맨 앞으로 보내기만 하면 되고, 대답은 there is/isn't/are/aren't로 하면 돼요.

A Fill in the blanks with *there is* or *there are*.

1. ___There is___ a computer in the room.   2. _____ two cars in the garage.

3. _____ some milk in the glass.   4. _____ a cell phone on the table.

5. _____ 500 Indian tribes in the U.S. 6. _____ four students in the library.

B Complete the conversations with *is*, *isn't*, *are*, or *aren't*.

1. A: ___Is___ there a movie ticket on the desk?
   B: No, there ___isn't___ .

2. A: _____ there a good view from the hotel?
   B: Yes, there _____ .

3. A: _____ there two cakes on the table?
   B: No, there _____ .

A Complete the questions. Then answer the questions as in the example.

1.

six students

_____Are there_____ five students in the classroom?

→ No, there aren't. There are six students in the classroom.

2.

digital camera

_____ a digital camera?

→ _____

3.

one woman

_____ two women in the restaurant?

→ _____

4.

fast food restaurant

_____ a shopping center in the street?

→ _____

B Make questions and give short answers.

1. Q: Is she a nurse? _____
   A: No, she isn't. _____ (She's not a nurse.)

2. Q: _____
   A: _____ (I'm not tired.)

3. Q: _____
   A: _____ (The students in this class are smart.)

C Read the information about Olivia below. Then complete the questions and answers.

Name: Olivia
Age: 13
Job: student
Nationality: Spanish
Look: pretty

1. ___Is she___ a teacher? → No, she isn't.
2. Is she young? → Yes, _____.
3. Is she Brazilian? → No, _____.
4. _____ Spanish? → Yes, she is.
5. _____ 13 years old? → Yes, she is.
6. Is she a student? → Yes, _____.
7. _____ ugly? → No, she isn't.
8. Is she pretty? → Yes, _____.

D Write sentences about the following people, as in the example. Use the information given.

1.
the USA
an actor
44 years old

David

David is from the USA.
He is an actor.
He is 44 years old.

2.
Korea
a cook
32 years old

Yeonsu

_____
_____
_____

3.
England
police officers
36 years old,
48 years old

Charlie and Harry

_____
_____
_____

E Look at Exercise D again and write three sentences about yourself.

1. _____
2. _____
3. _____

Ⓐ Look at the example and practice with a partner. (Repeat 3 times.)

1.

 Is Montel Smith a soccer player?

 No, he isn't. He is a baseball player.

1.

Montel Smith / a soccer player?
→ No / a baseball player

2.

Maria Fox / a nurse?
→ No / a doctor

3.

Matthew Wilson / an actor?
→ No / a singer

Ⓑ 다음은 서윤이의 교실을 묘사한 그림입니다. 아래의 주어진 어휘를 이용하여 교실에 있는 사람이나 사물을 there be를 써서 완전한 문장으로 말해 보세요.

There is a teacher in front of the blackboard.

Vocabulary Box			
on	behind	the desks	the wall	a/the blackboard
under	in front of	a/the teacher	a calendar	four students
		three schoolbags	a clock	books

Unit **2** **Simple Present 1**

Unit Focus
▶ Meaning & Uses of the Present Tense
▶ Negatives

Learn & Practice 1

Simple Present Tense

- 어제도, 오늘도, 내일도 있을 똑같은 일상적인 습관, 반복되는 동작에 현재 시제를 써요.

- 일반적인 사실, 과학적 사실이나 변하지 않는 진리에도 현재 시제를 씁니다.

Repeated Actions		True in General	
 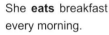			
She **eats** breakfast every morning.	We **walk** to school.	He **teaches** students.	Water **freezes** at zero degrees Celsius.

* 주어가 3인칭 단수(he, she, Scott, Kelly, a dog, it, etc.)일 때에만 동사 뒤에 -s나 -es를 붙여 3인칭 단수형 동사임을 알리는 표시를 해요.

* 주어가 복수 또는 I일 때에는 동사 뒤에 -s나 -es를 붙이지 않아요.

Subject	Verb	Subject	Verb
I/you we/they	read eat go watch	he/she/ it/Tom/ Olivia, etc.	read**s** eat**s** go**es** watch**es**

Ⓐ **Choose and write the correct forms of the verbs to describe the pictures. Use the simple present tense.**

brush	watch	take place	read	play	swim

1.
2.
3.

4.
5.
6.

1. Seo-yoon ___reads___ a book.

2. The girl _____ her teeth.

3. He _____ TV.

4. She _____ in the pool.

5. They _____ computer games.

6. The World Cup _____ every four years.

Spelling Rules of the Third-Person Singular

- 우리말과 다르게 영어에서는 3인칭 단수(he, she, it, Jane, etc.)일 경우 동사 뒤에 보통 -s나 -es를 붙여 주어가 3인칭 단수임을 알리자는 약속이 되어 있어요.

I study English.   You study English.   We study English.   They study English.

He **studies** English.   She **studies** English.   Peter **studies** English.   Lucy **studies** English.

-s	work → work**s** eat → eat**s** open → open**s** write → write**s**	• 대부분의 동사 끝에 -s를 붙임.
-es	watch → watch**es** wash → wash**es** fix → fix**es** go → go**es** pass → pass**es** mix → mix**es**	• -o, -s, -ch, -sh, -x로 끝나는 동사 뒤에 -es 붙이기
-ies	study → stud**ies** fly → fl**ies** cry → cr**ies**	• 『자음＋-y』로 끝나는 동사 → -y를 -i로 고치고 -es 붙이기
Irregular	have → **has**	• 불규칙 변화

A Underline the verb in each sentence. Add a final -s/-es to the verb.

1. Wood float on the water.
   floats

2. Ted go to the theater on Fridays.

3. He have some money.

4. My brother study very hard.

5. John brush his teeth before breakfast.

6. Eleanor try to pay attention in class.

7. My mom worry too much.

8. It cost a lot of money to have a pet.

Simple Present: Negatives

- 동사 바로 앞에 do not 또는 does not을 붙여 '~하지 않다, ~가 아니다'라는 뜻의 부정문을 만들어요. 주어가 3인칭 단수(he, she, it, Tom, etc.)일 때 동사 앞에 does not(=doesn't)을 써요. 이때 does가 3인칭을 알리는 역할을 하기 때문에 동사는 모양을 바꾸지 않고 동사 원형을 그대로 써야 해요.

He **doesn't like** jogging in the evenings.
He watches TV and eats doughnuts.

Jennifer **doesn't walk** to school.
She takes the school bus.

We **don't go** to the zoo.
We go to the park.

Affirmative					Negative			
I you we they	travel	he she it Tom	travels		I you we they	**don't travel**	he she it Mary	**doesn't travel**

* 일상 영어에서는 don't/doesn't와 같이 축약형을 많이 써요.

Ⓐ Write the negative as in the example.

1. She likes Japanese.
   → She doesn't like Japanese.

2. I ride my bike in the park.
   → _____

3. My parents go to the movie theater on Sundays.
   → _____

4. Ava watches horror films.
   → _____

5. Karen has breakfast with her family.
   → _____

A Look at the photos. Make positives or negatives.

1.

(a penguin / live in Africa)

A penguin doesn't live in Africa.

2.

(plants / need water to grow)

3.

(rice / grow on trees)

4.

(a chicken / give milk)

B The underlined words are incorrect. Correct and rewrite the paragraph.

Julie Darcy is a very famous music star. She sing, she plays the drums, and she's a great dancer, too. Julie is an amazing drummer and she's only 10 years old! In her free time she like going out with her friends, but she don't have much free time. Every day she go to school, and then she have after-school activities.

Julie Darcy is a very famous music star. She sings, she plays the drums, and she's a great dancer, too.

C Read the above paragraph again and answer the questions.

1. Who's Julie Darcy? →

2. What musical instrument does she play? →

3. What does she like in her free time? →

D Choose one verb to make each sentence negative.

1. It _____doesn't snow_____ very often in Busan.
   (snow, sing, play)

2. Olivia lives in Korea, but she _____ a word of Korean.   (sing, work, speak)

cricket

3. I'm sorry - I _____ your name.
              (eat, remember, work)

4. Kelly is really tired, but she _____ to go to bed.
                    (help, want, walk)

5. He likes football, but he _____ cricket at all.
              (think, like, remember)

E Complete the sentences as in the example.

1.
I don't drink coffee.
I drink milk.

Jennifer _doesn't drink coffee. She drinks milk._

2.
I don't do exercise.
I do my homework every day.

Amy _____

_____

3.
I don't ride my skateboard.
I ride my bicycle.

Jack _____

_____

4.
I don't watch TV on Thursdays.
I watch DVDs on Thursdays.

William _____

_____

A Look at the example and practice with a partner. (Repeat 3 times.)

1.

Kathy gets up at 6:00.

She doesn't get up at 7:00.

1.

Kathy

get up at 6:00 (O)

get up at 7:00 (X)

2.

my dog

like meat (O)

like fish (X)

3.

Lucy

read books (O)

read comic books (X)

4.

Mina

study English (O)

study Japanese (X)

B What do you do in the summer? Say five things you do and five things you don't do.

In the summer I go to the beach with my family. I don't go to school.

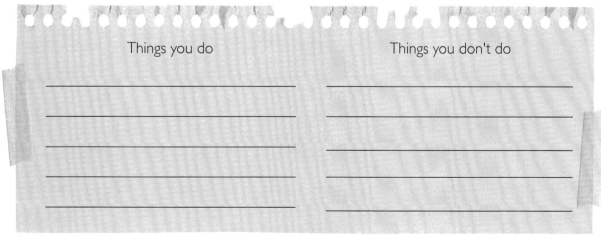

Things you do	Things you don't do
_____	_____
_____	_____
_____	_____
_____	_____
_____	_____

Unit **3** **Simple Present 2**

⊕ **Unit Focus**
▶ Yes/No Questions
▶ Asking Information Questions

Simple Present: *Yes/No* questions

- 의문문을 만들 때에는 do 또는 does를 문장 맨 앞에 쓰고 물음표를 붙여요. 우리말로 '~하니, ~이니?'라는 뜻이지요.

- 주어가 3인칭 단수(he, she, it, Tom, etc.)인 경우에만 does를 써요.

Q: **Does** Jessica jog every morning?
A: **Yes**, she **does**.

Q: **Do** you like Justin Bieber?
A: **No, I don't.** I like Jay-Z.

Subject	Questions	Answers	
I/you/we/they	**Do** you...?	**Yes**, I do.	**No**, I don't.
he/she/it 등 3인칭 단수	**Does** he...?	**Yes**, he does.	**No**, he doesn't.

- 의문문에 대한 대답은 do/does로 대답해요. 짧게 대답할 수도 있고, yes/no 뒤에 긴 대답을 붙여서 말할 수도 있어요.

Do you learn yoga these days?

→ Yes, I do.　　OR　　Yes, I learn yoga these days.

Ⓐ Read and put in *do* or *does*.

1. __Do__ you know my friend Andy?

2. _____ this bus go to Cambridge?

3. _____ Sarah go to school on Saturdays?

4. _____ Bill and Harry play golf?

5. _____ she want to come with us?

6. _____ they speak Korean?

Ⓑ Make questions and match them to their answers.

1. Tom drinks milk every day. _____*Does Tom drink milk every day?*_____ •　• a. Yes, she does.

2. Ann teaches French. _____ •　• b. No, they don't.

3. Bob and Kevin play baseball. _____ •　• c. Yes, he does.

Simple Present: Information Questions with *Where*

- 궁금한 것이 '장소'나 '위치'일 때 의문사 where를 문장 맨 앞에 써요. 구체적인 정보를 물어보기 때문에 yes나 no로 대답하지 않아요.
- 'Where + do/does + 주어 + 동사 원형…?'의 어순으로 써요. 주어가 3인칭 단수인 경우에만 does를 써요.

Do penguins live in the Antarctic?
　　　　→ Yes, they do.
Where do penguins live?
　　　　　→ (They live) In the Antarctic.

Does Tom work in a bank?　　→ Yes, he does.
Where does Tom work?　　→ (He works) In a bank.

A Circle the correct words.

1. Where (do / (does)) Jane ((come) / comes) from?

2. Where (do / does) Tom (live / lives)?

3. Where (do / does) they (go / goes)?

4. Where (do / does) Jim and Sunny (go / goes) after school?

5. Where (do / does) you (want / wants) to eat?

B Make sentences as in the example.

1. where + Your brother sleeps. 　→ 　*Where does your brother sleep?*

2. where + You play soccer. 　→ 　_____

3. where + Tom eats lunch every day. 　→ 　_____

4. where + Steve waits for the bus. 　→ 　_____

Simple Present: Information Questions with *What*

- 궁금한 것이 '무엇, 어떤 것'일 때 의문사 what을 문장 맨 앞에 써서 의문문을 만들어요. 구체적인 정보를 물어보기 때문에 yes나 no로 대답하지 않아요.
- 'what + do/does + 주어 + 동사 원형…?'의 어순으로 써요. 주어가 3인칭 단수인 경우에만 does를 써요.

	Do/Does	Subject	Base Verb
What	do	I/you/we/they	like...?
	does	he/she/it/Tom, etc.	

- 'What + do/does + 주어 + do?'는 직업을 묻는 질문이에요.

A Complete the sentences with *What do* or *What does* and match them to their answers.

1. ___What does___ he teach?   • a. They like hiking.

2. _____ Jane have for lunch?   • b. She plays the guitar.

3. _____ she play?   • c. She prepares breakfast in the morning.

4. _____ they like?   • d. He teaches French.

5. _____ your mom do   • e. She has French fries.
   in the morning?

A Write *do* or *does* to complete the questions and *do*, *don't*, *does*, or *doesn't* to complete the short answers.

1. Q: ___Does___ she live with her parents?   A: Yes, she ___does___ .

2. Q: _____ you like your job?   A: No, I _____ .

3. Q: _____ I speak Italian well?   A: Yes, you _____ .

4. Q: _____ your sister visit you very often?   A: Yes, she _____ .

5. Q: _____ Olivia help you very much?   A: Yes, she _____ .

B Make questions as in the examples.

1. Q: *Does Janet eat lunch at the cafeteria every day?*
   A: Yes, she does. (Janet eats lunch at the cafeteria every day.)

2. Q: *Where does Janet eat lunch every day?*
   A: At the cafeteria. (Janet eats lunch at the cafeteria every day.)

3. Q: _____
   A: Yes, he does. (Richard eats dinner at a restaurant every day.)

4. Q: _____
   A: At a restaurant. (Richard eats dinner at a restaurant every day.)

5. Q: _____
   A: Yes, she does. (Hyemi works at a broadcasting station.)

6. Q: _____
   A: At a broadcasting station. (Hyemi works at a broadcasting station.)

7. Q: _____
   A: Yes, they do. (Firefighters work at a fire station.)

8. Q: _____
   A: At a fire station. (Firefighters work at a fire station.)

C Write questions and answers using the simple present, as in the example.

1. The shop / close / at 8:00 p.m. / on Saturday.   (close at 9:00 p.m.)

   Q: *Does the shop close at 8:00 p.m. on Saturday?*

   A: *No, the shop doesn't close at 8:00 p.m. on Saturday. It closes at 9:00 p.m.*

2. Ms. Lane / like / ice cream   (like banana cake)

   Q: _____

   A: _____

3. Tom's father / work / on the weekend.   (play sports)

   Q: _____

   A: _____

4. Sandy / clean / the house / on Friday.   (wash the car)

   Q: _____

   A: _____

D Look at the pictures and write questions and answers, as in the example.

1.

   What / Ava / do / in the afternoon?
   → watch TV

   What does Ava do in the afternoon?

   She watches TV.

2.

   What / Jason / do / on Sundays?
   → play computer games

   _____

   _____

E Answer the questions about yourself.

1. Do you like sports?

   _____

2. Do you go to a movie theater on Saturdays?

   _____

3. Do you watch horror films on TV?

   _____

4. Do you like reading books?

   _____

A Look at the example and practice with a partner. (Repeat 3 times.)

1.

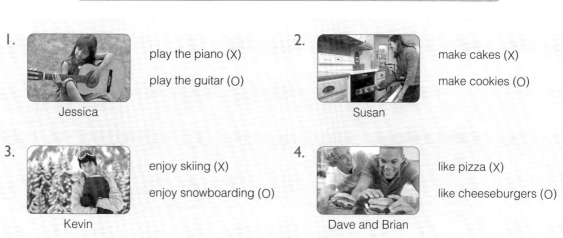

Does Jessica play the piano? No, she doesn't.

What does she play? She plays the guitar.

1.
play the piano (X)
play the guitar (O)
Jessica

2.
make cakes (X)
make cookies (O)
Susan

3.
enjoy skiing (X)
enjoy snowboarding (O)
Kevin

4.
like pizza (X)
like cheeseburgers (O)
Dave and Brian

B Ask your partner questions using *where*. Use the words and phrases below or invent your own.

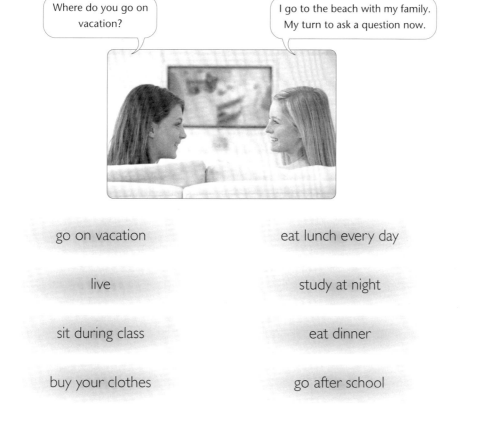

Where do you go on vacation?

I go to the beach with my family. My turn to ask a question now.

go on vacation   eat lunch every day

live   study at night

sit during class   eat dinner

buy your clothes   go after school

Present Progressive: Affirmative Statements

- 현재 진행 시제는 우리가 말하는 순간, 또는 보고 있는 그 순간에 진행 중인 동작이나 행동을 나타내요. 'be 동사(am, is, are) + v-ing' 형태로 만들고 이것은 우리말로 '~하고 있다, ~하고 있는 중이다'라는 뜻이 되지요.

Cindy **is holding** an umbrella.
It **is raining** now.

Kathy and Tom **are sitting**.
They **are waiting** for a train.

- 진행형의 형태는 'be + -ing'로 주어가 단수일 때 is, 주어가 복수일 때에는 are를 써요.

Subject	Be Verb	Verb + *-ing*
I	am	
He/She/It	is	work**ing**.
You/We/They	are	

A Look at the pictures. Write the correct sentences in the blanks.

Nancy is riding her bicycle.   Those girls are taking a picture.

She is drinking water.

1. She is drinking water.   2. _____   3. _____

Present Progressive: Spelling Rules of Verb-*ing*

- 'be + v-ing' 형태에서 동사에 -ing를 붙여 만드는 몇 가지 규칙만 알면 쉬워요.

Ava **is smiling**.

She **is sitting** on a chair.

She **is working** on her computer.

Rules   **Examples**

• 대부분의 동사는 동사 원형에 -ing를 붙여요.	talk → talk**ing** read → read**ing** walk → walk**ing** play → play**ing** go → go**ing** sleep → sleep**ing** draw → draw**ing** drink → drink**ing**

• -e로 끝나는 동사는 -e를 없애고 -ing를 붙여요.	come → com**ing** smile → smil**ing** dance → danc**ing** make → mak**ing**

• '단모음 + 단자음'으로 끝나는 동사는 마지막 자음을 한 번 더 쓰고 -ing를 붙여요.	sit → sit**ting** get → get**ting** run → run**ning** swim → swim**ming** cut → cut**ting** stop → stop**ping**

Ⓐ Use the rules for adding -*ing* to the verbs in the box. Then write them in the correct column.

repair	wear	put	move	hope	dance
play	wash	get	stop	read	smile
save	swim	cut			

Add -*ing*	Drop -e and add -*ing*	Double the consonant, add -*ing*
playing	saving	getting
_____	_____	_____
_____	_____	_____
_____	_____	_____
_____	_____	_____

Present Progressive: Negatives

- 현재진행형의 부정문은 be 동사의 부정문과 마찬가지로 be 동사 바로 뒤에 not만 붙이면 돼요. 우리말로 '~하고 있지 않다'라는 뜻이 됩니다.

Kelly **isn't playing** the drums.
She is playing the violin.

They **aren't watching** TV.
They are having dinner.

Samuel **isn't talking** on the phone.
He is listening to music.

- 부정문에서는 주로 축약형을 많이 써요. 축약형은 두 가지 형태가 있어요.

I	**am not** / 'm not	
He/She/It	**is not** / 's not / isn't	**-ing**.
You/We/They	**are not** / 're not / aren't	

She is not sleeping. = She**'s not** sleeping. = She **isn't** sleeping.

A Make positives (P) and negatives (N). Use the present progressive.

1. Nancy sleeps.
   → (P) _____Nancy is sleeping._____
   → (N) _____Nancy isn't sleeping._____

2. Tom drinks milk.
   → (P) _____
   → (N) _____

3. They play badminton.
   → (P) _____
   → (N) _____

B Look at the pictures and fill in the blanks.

1.

   He ___isn't playing___ badminton.
   He is playing tennis.

2.

   Kathy _____ a horse.
   She is riding her bicycle.

3.

   Mark _____ any books.
   He is buying some toys.

A Look at the pictures and write sentences as in the example.

1. Shh! The baby is sleeping.

play

No, he isn't sleeping.

He is playing.

2. Look! The woman is eating.

drink / water

_____

_____

3. Be quiet. Cindy is working.

eat / a hamburger

_____

_____

4. Edward is sitting under a tree.

climb / a tree

_____

_____

5. Look! Those girls are taking a picture.

walk / to school

_____

_____

6. Tom is talking on the phone.

take / a shower

_____

_____

B Look at the pictures in each question. Make positives and negatives.

1.

(X)   (O)

→ They aren't playing basketball.

→ They are playing soccer.

2.

(X)   (O)

→ _____

→ _____

3.

(X)   (O)

→ _____

→ _____

C Look at the picture and write sentences using the words from the boxes.

Nouns: her phone   a chair   his laptop
        blue jeans   her credit card
        a white dress   a striped shirt

Verbs: hold   speak   wear   sit
        look at   work

1. The woman is speaking on her phone.
2. _____
3. _____
4. _____
5. _____
6. _____
7. _____
8. _____

A Look at the example and practice with a partner. (Repeat 3 times.)

I.

 Thomas isn't working in the garden.

 He is washing the dishes now.

I.
Thomas

work in the garden (X)

wash the dishes now (O)

2.
Michelle

learn math now (X)

play the flute now (O)

3.
Rachel and her friends

ride their bicycles (X)

take a picture (O)

4.
Kevin and Heather

swim in the sea (X)

make sandcastles (O)

B Work with a partner. Make sentences about your classmates' activities right now.

In the first picture, Jane is reading a book, but in the second picture, she isn't reading a book. She is listening to music. Your turn now.

In the first...

Present Progressive 2

Unit Focus
- ▶ *Yes/No* Questions
- ▶ Future Plans
- ▶ Information Questions

Present Progressive: *Yes/No* Questions

- 우리말로 '~하고 있니?, ~하고 있는 중이니?'라는 뜻은 be 동사를 문장 맨 앞으로 보내고 물음표(?)를 붙이면 돼요. 대답도 yes/no를 이용해 알맞은 be 동사로 대답하지요.

Statement

William is washing his car right now.

Question

Is William wash**ing** his car right now?
→ **Yes**, he **is**. (He's washing his car.)
→ **No**, he **isn't**. (He's not washing his car.)

Statement

The children are playing in the park.

Question

Are the children play**ing** in the park?
→ **Yes**, they **are**. (They're playing in the park.)
→ **No**, they **aren't**. (They're not playing in the park.)

- no로 대답할 때에는 주로 축약형을 쓰지만, yes로 대답할 때에는 축약형을 쓰지 않아요.

Be Verb	Subject	V-*ing*?
Am	I	
Is	he/she/it/Tom, etc.	sleep**ing**?
Are	you/we/they, etc.	

A Change the sentences to questions and complete the short answers.

1. She is working hard. _____Is she working hard?_____ No, _____she isn't_____.

2. They are writing a composition. _____ Yes, _____.

3. He is cutting the cake. _____ No, _____.

Present Progressive as a Future Tense

- 이미 정해져 있는 일정은 현재진행형으로 미래를 나타낼 수 있어요. 주로 시간을 나타내는 표현과 자주 쓰여요.
- 주로 움직임을 나타내는 come, go, stay, arrive, leave나 교통수단을 나타내는 fly, walk, ride, drive, take 등이 자주 쓰여요.

Olivia's schedule for next week

on Monday afternoon

→ She **is playing** tennis on Monday afternoon.

on Friday

→ She **is going** to the movies on Friday.

on Saturday

→ She **is having** dinner with her friends on Saturday.

Ⓐ Are the following sentences present or future? Write *present* or *future* after each one.

1. I'm seeing Ava on Wednesday.   →   *future*

2. Where is Sunny? Is she working?   →   *present*

3. Are you going out tonight?   → _____

4. That tree's growing very fast.   → _____

5. I'm waiting for a call at the moment.   → _____

6. We're getting a new car next week.   → _____

7. My parents are coming to stay with me this weekend.   → _____

Present Progressive: Information Questions

- '무엇'이 궁금하여 물어볼 때 what을 써요. what은 우리말로 '무엇을'을 뜻하며 'What + be 동사 + 주어 + v-ing'의 어순으로 써요. who는 '누가'라는 뜻으로 문장에서 주어 역할도 해요.

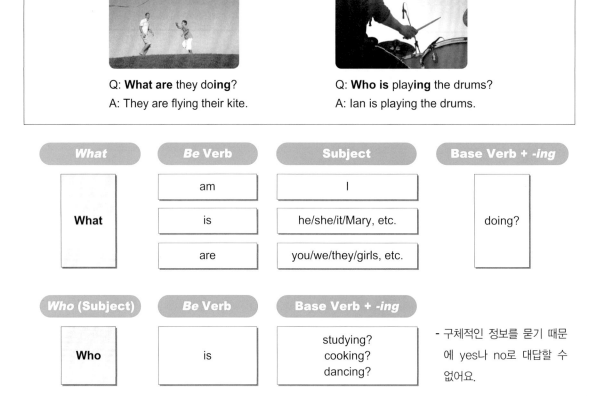

Q: **What are** they do**ing**?
A: They are flying their kite.

Q: **Who is** play**ing** the drums?
A: Ian is playing the drums.

What	Be Verb	Subject	Base Verb + -ing
What	am is are	I he/she/it/Mary, etc. you/we/they/girls, etc.	doing?

Who (Subject)	Be Verb	Base Verb + -ing	
Who	is	studying? cooking? dancing?	- 구체적인 정보를 묻기 때문에 yes나 no로 대답할 수 없어요.

A Complete the questions and match them to their answers.

1. ___Who___ is cleaning the room? •
   • a. She's speaking on the phone and walking.

2. _____ is the man doing? •
   • b. Kathy is cleaning the room.

3. _____ is the woman doing? •
   • c. He's listening to music.

4. _____ is walking to school? •
   • d. Tom and Jane are walking to school.

A Look at the pictures. Write questions and answers.

1.

they / study / English / at a language school?
→ No / take a picture

Q: Are they studying English at a language school?

A: No, they aren't. They are taking a picture.

2.

they / wait for / the train?
→ No / study in the library

Q: _____

A: _____

3.

Jane / listen to / music?
→ No / take the subway

Q: _____

A: _____

B Look at the pictures and write questions or answers, as in the examples.

1.

Mary

2.

have dinner

3.

Martin

4.

paint the house

5.

Bob

6.

take Taekwondo lessons

1. Q: Who is waiting for the train?

   A: Mary is waiting for the train.

2. Q: What are they doing?

   A: They are having dinner.

3. Q: _____

   A: Martin is climbing the tree.

4. Q: What are they doing?

   A: _____

5. Q: _____

   A: Bob is taking off the clothes.

6. Q: What are they doing?

   A: _____

C Complete the conversation using the information in the diary. Use verbs in the present continuous and add any other words you need.

Monday	7 p.m. - Movie Theater - with Cindy
Tuesday	
Wednesday	Family Restaurant
Thursday	
Friday	Meet Peter - Airport - 8:00
Saturday	Visit Museum - with Peter
Sunday	

A: What ~~are you doing~~ on Monday night? (you / do)

B: ~~I'm going to the movie theater.~~ (I / go)

A: Who _____ with? (you / go)

B: _____ (I / go / with)

A: What time _____ her? (you / meet)

B: At 7 o'clock.

A: And what about on Wednesday? _____ _____? (you / go out)

B: Yes, I am. I'm going to a family restaurant.

A: _____ at home on Friday? (you / stay)

B: No, I _____. (meet)

A: What time _____? (he / arrive)

B: At 8:00.

A: Are you staying at home on Saturday?

B: No, _____. (we / visit)

D Read the dialog below and make questions and answers to describe the picture.

Dad : Hi, Kevin. How are you doing?

Kevin: Fine. How about you?

Dad: Good. How's everyone?

Kevin: They're doing fine.

Dad: What are you doing, Kevin?

Kevin: ~~I'm watching TV.~~

Dad: What is Jennifer doing?

Kevin: _____

Dad: _____

Kevin: Bob (= He) _____.

Dad: _____

Kevin: Grandfather (= He) _____.

A Look at the example and practice with a partner. (Repeat 3 times.)

1.

 Is Tom riding a horse?   No, he isn't.

 What is he doing?   He is driving a car.

1.

drive / a car

Tom

ride a horse (X)

2.

sleep

Mr. Parker

work (X)

3.

sunbathe

John

sleep (X)

4.

take / photos

Kathy and Susan

talk on the phone (X)

5.

play / the guitar

Kevin

play football (X)

6.

cook

Ava

clean the kitchen (X)

B Answer each question with a complete sentence.

1.

What are they doing?

2.

What is he doing?

They are fishing.

3.

What are they doing?

4.

What is the boy doing?

5.

What is she doing?

Unit **6** **Nouns, Articles**

Unit Focus
▶ Nouns   ▶ Singular & Plural
▶ Article *A* or *An*   ▶ Irregular Plural Nouns

Learn & Practice 1

Nouns

- 명사(nouns)는 사람, 사물, 장소, 생각 등을 나타내는 단어입니다.

- 명사는 크게 보통 명사(common nouns)와 고유 명사(proper nouns)로 나뉘는데, 보통 명사는 우리 눈에 보이는 모든 이름을 가진 명사를 말해요.

- 고유 명사는 사람, 지역, 나라 등의 이름을 나타내는 특별한 명사라 하여 고유 명사라고 해요. 고유 명사의 첫 글자는 항상 대문자로 써야 해요.

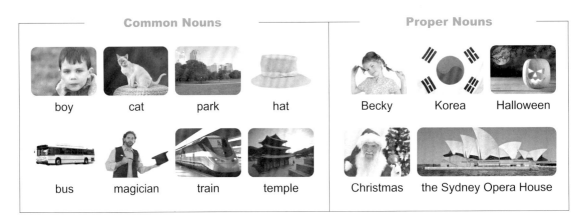

Common Nouns	Proper Nouns
boy cat park hat	Becky Korea Halloween
bus magician train temple	Christmas the Sydney Opera House

A Write each common noun under the correct heading.

theater   lion   girl   brother   doctor   restaurant
elephant   kangaroo   museum   book   computer   desk

people	animals	places	things
girl			

B Underline the common nouns and circle the proper nouns in these sentences.

1. (Kim) and (Stephanie) wore masks on (Halloween).

2. The tourists visited Rome and saw the Colosseum.

The Indefinite Article: *A/An*

- '하나, 한 명'이라는 개념으로 셀 수 있는 단수 명사 앞에 쓰는 a/an을 부정관사라고 해요.
- 대부분의 명사 앞에 'a'를 쓰지만, 첫소리가 모음(a, e, i, o, u)으로 발음되는 명사 앞에는 'an'을 써요.

	Using *A*			Using *An*	
a ball	**a** teacher	**a** car	**an** airplane	**an** island	**an** umbrella

A Complete the sentences. Use *a* or *an*.

1. Are you going on ___*a*___ vacation this summer?

2. _____ elephant is a big animal.

3. Julie has got _____ orange.

4. There are 24 hours in _____ day.

5. I don't have _____ car or _____ apartment.

6. Look! That's _____ eagle. It's in the sky.

Singular and Plural Nouns

- 명사의 복수형은 셀 수 있는 명사로 하나, 둘, 셋, 넷 등으로 셀 수 있으며, 명사 뒤에 -s, -es 또는 -ies를 붙여서 복수형을 만들어요.

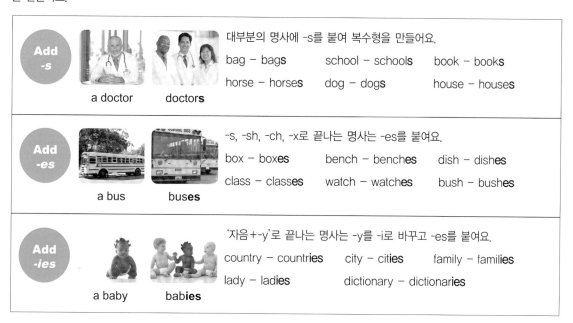

Add -s

a doctor   doctor**s**

대부분의 명사에 -s를 붙여 복수형을 만들어요.

| bag – bag**s** | school – school**s** | book – book**s** |
| horse – horse**s** | dog – dog**s** | house – house**s** |

Add -es

a bus   bus**es**

-s, -sh, -ch, -x로 끝나는 명사는 -es를 붙여요.

| box – box**es** | bench – bench**es** | dish – dish**es** |
| class – class**es** | watch – watch**es** | bush – bush**es** |

Add -ies

a baby   bab**ies**

'자음+-y'로 끝나는 명사는 -y를 -i로 바꾸고 -es를 붙여요.

| country – countr**ies** | city – cit**ies** | family – famil**ies** |
| lady – lad**ies** | dictionary – dictionar**ies** | |

 Write the plural of the following words.

1. leaf → _leaves_

2. lady → _____

3. school → _____

4. forest → _____

5. bus → _____

6. bookcase → _____

7. family → _____

8. bush → _____

9. bench → _____

Learn & Practice 4

Irregular Plural Nouns

- 명사에 -(e)s를 붙이는 것처럼 일정한 규칙이 없이 자체의 복수형을 가지거나 단수와 복수형의 모양이 똑같은 불규칙 명사들도 있어요.

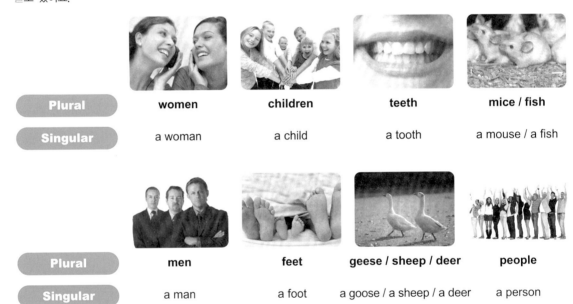

| Plural | women | children | teeth | mice / fish |
| Singular | a woman | a child | a tooth | a mouse / a fish |

| Plural | men | feet | geese / sheep / deer | people |
| Singular | a man | a foot | a goose / a sheep / a deer | a person |

Ⓐ Read and complete the sentences using the plural form.

1. Kathy has one child. Smith has two ___children___ .

2. Eric has one fish in his aquarium. Cindy has five _____ in her aquarium.

3. I have a right and left foot. I have two _____.

4. There's one goose near the lake. There are a lot of _____ over there.

5. There's one woman in our home. There are ten _____ in your home.

6. There's one mouse in this box. There are five _____ in that box.

A Write the plural form of each noun on the line.

| baby | butterfly | city | country |

1. ___babies___   2. _____   3. _____   4. _____

| dictionary | discovery | lady | library | party |

5. _____   6. _____   7. _____   8. _____   9. _____

B Fill in the blanks with singular or plural nouns.

1.
There is one ___child___ in the classroom. There are three ___children___ on the playground. How many ___children___ are on the playground? There are three ___children___ on the playground. How many ___children___ are in the classroom? There is ___one___ ___child___ in the classroom.

2.
There is one mouse in the house. There are twenty _____ in the field. How many _____ are in the field? There are twenty _____ in the field. How many _____ are in the house? There is _____ in the house.

3.
There is one woman in the office. There are nine _____ in the supermarket. How many _____ are in the supermarket? There are nine _____ in the supermarket. How many _____ are in the office? There is _____ in the office.

4.
Tom had an accident and lost a tooth. The dentist pulled out all of my grandfather's _____. How many of my grandfather's _____ did the dentist pull out? The dentist pulled out all of my grandfather's _____. How many _____ did Tom lose in an accident? Tom lost _____ in an accident.

C Write about these people.

Eva

Ellen

Steve

You

	Eva	Ellen	Steve	You
Nationality	French	Swedish	American	_____
Job	fashion model	architect	electrician	_____
Hair	black	blond	black	_____
Eyes	brown	blue	grey	_____
Abilities	dance, swim	play tennis, sing	drive, play baseball	_____

1. Eva   is French. She is a fashion model. She has got black hair and brown eyes. She can dance and swim.

2. Ellen   _____

_____

3. Steve   _____

_____

4. I   _____

_____

D Choose and make sentences with *a* or *an*.

engineer   auto mechanic   taxi driver   firefighter

1.

Q: What does he do?
A: _He is a taxi driver._

2.

Q: What does he do?
A: _____

3.

Q: What does she do?
A: _____

4.

Q: What does he do?
A: _____

A Look at the example and practice with a partner. (Repeat 3 times.)

1.

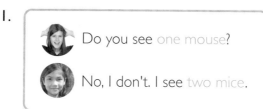

> Do you see one mouse?
>
> No, I don't. I see two mice.

1. one mouse (X) / two (O)

2. one puppy (X) / three (O)

3. one sheep (X) / five (O)

4. one lady (X) / two (O)

5. one child (X) / four (O)

6. three fish (X) / five (O)

B Talk about what you see. Use *a* or *an* if you're talking about just one thing.

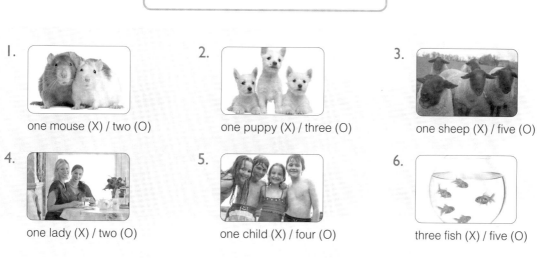

> I (can) see an umbrella in the store.

> Your turn now.

Ⓧ **Unit Focus**
- ▶ Subject Pronouns
- ▶ Object Pronouns
- ▶ Demonstratives

Subject Pronouns

- 대명사는 명사를 대신해서 쓰는 말이에요. 사람, 동물, 사물, 장소 등을 대신한다고 하여 대명사라고 불러요.

- 대명사가 문장에서 주어 자리에 있는 명사를 대신할 수 있는 자격이 있다고 하여 주격 대명사라고 불러요.

The girl is Cindy.	The car is expensive.	My parents are doctors.	The horses are fast.
= **She** is a student.	= **It** is expensive.	= **They** are doctors.	= **They** are fast.

	Singular	**Plural**
people(사람)	I, you, he, she	we, you, they
animal(동물), thing(사물), place(장소)	it	they

Ⓐ **Write the correct subject pronouns.**

1. Mary and Bob → _they_

2. Olivia and I → _____

3. Kathy and you → _____

4. a smartphone → _____

5. bicycles → _____

6. people → _____

7. a T-shirt → _____

8. Anna → _____

Ⓑ **Choose the correct subject pronouns.**

1. This is my umbrella. (I / It) is yellow.

2. This is Eric. (She / He) is my friend.

3. This is Laura and Rose. (They / She) are my friends.

4. This is my notebook. (It / We) is blue.

Object Pronouns

- 대명사가 문장에서 목적어로 쓰이면 목적격(목적어 자격) 대명사라고 해요.
- 전치사 뒤에 대명사를 쓸 경우에도 대명사의 목적격을 써야 해요.

I really like Jenny.
= I really like **her**.

Lisa works with William.
= Lisa works with **him**.

He repairs the car.
= He repairs **it**.

I like vegetables.
= I like **them**.

	Singular	**Plural**
people(사람)	me, you, him, her	us, you, them
animal(동물), thing(사물), place(장소)	it	them

Ⓐ Complete the sentences with an object pronoun.

1. Peter is a very nice man. Do you know _____*him*_____ ?

2. I can't open this door. Could you open _____ for me, please?

3. Those shoes are really nice. I'd like to buy _____ .

4. I can't do this homework. Can you help _____ ?

5. She speaks very quickly. I can't understand _____ .

Ⓑ Change the sentences using object pronouns.

1. He calls Mary.   → He calls ____*her*____ .

2. You eat breakfast with David.   → You eat breakfast with _____ .

3. She wants the book.   → She wants _____ .

4. Max likes David and me.   → Max likes _____ .

5. We love to meet Peter and Julie. → We love to meet _____ .

Demonstratives

- 이것(this), 저것(that)처럼 손가락으로 지시하듯이 가리키며 사용하는 대명사를 지시대명사라고 해요.

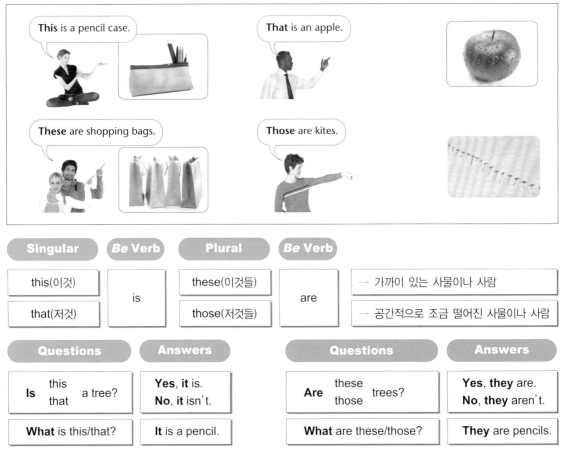

Singular	Be Verb	Plural	Be Verb	
this(이것)	is	these(이것들)	are	→ 가까이 있는 사물이나 사람
that(저것)		those(저것들)		→ 공간적으로 조금 떨어진 사물이나 사람

Questions	Answers	Questions	Answers
Is this / that a tree?	**Yes**, it is. / **No**, it isn't.	**Are** these / those trees?	**Yes**, they are. / **No**, they aren't.
What is this/that?	**It** is a pencil.	**What** are these/those?	**They** are pencils.

- 의문문에 대한 대답은 지시대명사를 쓰지 않고 단수일 때에는 it, 복수일 때에는 they를 써서 답해요.

A Choose the correct words.

1. (Those / These) are sunflowers.

2. (Those / That) are ice skates.

3. A: Is this a flute?
   B: No, (it / they) is a guitar.

4. (These / Those) (is / are) coins.

5. A: What are (this / these)?
   B: (It / They) are rings.

A Replace the underlined words with a subject or object pronoun.

1. Ms. Ava is our English teacher.
   → She is our English teacher.

2. She uses this book to teach grammar.
   → _____

3. My friends and I study English at the same school.
   → _____

4. She teaches the students and me grammar.
   → _____

5. The students like Ms. Ava.
   → _____

6. The students ask her questions.
   → _____

7. She answers the questions.
   → _____

8. Olivia always asks questions.
   → _____

B Write answers using a subject or object pronoun.

Questions

1. What time is the next train?
   → (9:00 / leaves / at)

2. Where is William?
   → (has moved / Seattle / to)

3. Have you seen my dictionaries?
   → (on / the table / are)

4. What do you think of my new sunglasses?
   → (like)

5. What is Olivia doing this summer?
   → (France / to / travel / is)

6. I'm learning Japanese. Is it easy?
   → (No / difficult / is)

Answers

1. It leaves at 9:00.

2. _____

3. _____

4. _____

5. _____

6. _____

C Look at the pictures and make sentences as in the examples. Use *this*, *these*, *that*, or *those*.

1.

That is a mountain.

2.

These are horses.

3.

_____

4.

_____

5.

_____

6.

_____

D Look at the pictures and complete the sentences.

1. ___Are those___ books?   ___No, they aren't.___
    ___They are watermelons.___

(watermelon)

2. _____ a dog?   _____

    _____

(wolf)

3. _____ eagles?   _____

    _____

(ostrich)

A Look at the example and practice with a partner. (Repeat 3 times.)

1.

What is this? Is it an MP3 player?

No, it is a smartphone.

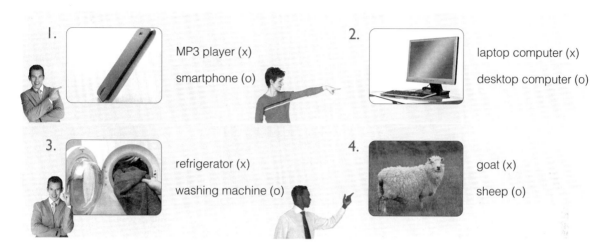

1. MP3 player (x)

smartphone (o)

2. laptop computer (x)

desktop computer (o)

3. refrigerator (x)

washing machine (o)

4. goat (x)

sheep (o)

B Work in pairs. Point to objects near or far from you and make sentences. Don't use a dictionary.

This is a desktop computer.
Those are science books.

C Bring a newspaper with photos (or photos of your family or friends) to class. Work with a partner. Look at the pictures. You says, *This is...* OR *These are....* Your partner says another thing using a pronoun.

This is my father.
He is a firefighter.

This is Patricia
She is an actress.

Possessives

Possessive Adjectives

- 소유형용사는 '소유형용사 + 명사'로 써서 '~의 명사'라는 뜻의 소유를 나타내요. 소유격은 항상 뒤에 명사가 함께 와야 해요.

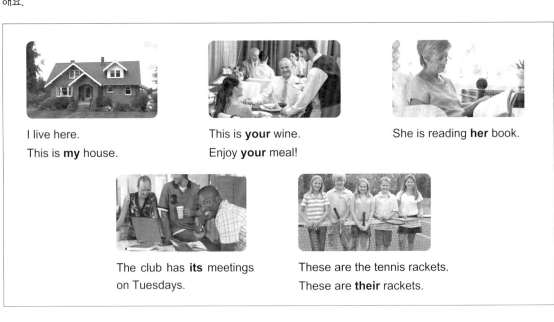

I live here.
This is **my** house.

This is **your** wine.
Enjoy **your** meal!

She is reading **her** book.

The club has **its** meetings on Tuesdays.

These are the tennis rackets.
These are **their** rackets.

주격	I	we	you	he	she	it	they
소유격	**my** (나의)	**our** (우리들의)	**your** (너의, 너희들의)	**his** (그의)	**her** (그녀의)	**its** (그것의)	**their** (그들의)

＊ it is의 축약형인 it's와 it의 소유격인 its를 혼동하지 마세요.

Ⓐ Look at the pictures and write as in the example.

1.

I have a handkerchief.
It's ___my handkerchief___ .

2.

She has a scarf.
It's _____ .

3.

They have a car.
It's _____ .

Possessive Nouns

- 명사의 소유격은 명사 뒤에 apostrophe(')와 -s를 붙여서 만들어요. 단수 명사와 불규칙 복수 명사는 명사에 -'s를 붙이기만 하면 돼요.
- -s로 끝나는 복수 명사에는 apostrophe(')만 붙여 소유격을 만들어요.

My **friend's** car is red.

children**'s** books	men**'s** clothing
people**'s** lives	teachers**'** office
John**'s** bag	the girl**'s** name
sharks**'** teeth	the cat**'s** tail
the man**'s** hat	runners**'** shoes

The store sells **women's** shoes.

A Make -'s or -s' possessive structures.

1. The dog belongs to Joe. → *Joe's dog*

2. The house belongs to Ann. → _____

3. The book belongs to the girls. → _____

4. The money belongs to the children. → _____

5. The hat belongs to the man. → _____

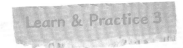

Possessive Pronouns

- 소유대명사는 '~의 것'이라는 뜻으로 쓰이며 단독으로 명사 역할을 할 수 있어요. 뒤에 명사를 쓰지 않으며, '소유형용사 + 명사'와 같은 뜻이므로 바꿔 쓸 수 있어요.

This is my backpack.
This backpack is **mine**.

That is her tennis racquet.
That tennis racquet is **hers**.

These are their skateboards.
These skateboards are **theirs**.

This is his guitar.
This guitar is **his**.

Possessive Pronouns

my book	= mine
your book	= yours
his book	= his
her book	= hers
their book	= theirs

- its는 소유형용사로서 뒤에 명사가 와야 하고 소유대명사로는 쓰지 않아요.

A Complete the sentences with the correct possessive pronouns.

1. Where is my smartphone? I can't find _mine_ .

2. Are they her sneakers? Yes, the shoes are _____ .

3. That's not his book. _____ is thick.

4. Can we use your telephone? _____ aren't working.

5. This is your socks. Take _____ .

Questions with *Whose*

- whose는 바로 뒤에 명사를 써서 '누구의'란 뜻의 형용사처럼 쓰기도 하고, 뒤에 명사를 쓰지 않고 단독으로 '누구의 것' 이란 뜻의 대명사처럼 쓰기도 해요.
- 대답할 때에는 누구의 것인지를 물어보는 말이므로 소유형용사 또는 소유대명사를 이용해서 대답해요.

Q: **Whose laptop** is that?
A: It is **her** laptop.

Q: **Whose** is that laptop?
A: It is **hers**.

Questions	Answers with Possessives
Whose dog is this? **Whose** is this?	It's **Nancy's** (= Nancy's dog). It's **her** dog. It's **hers**.
Whose books are those? **Whose** are those?	They're **Peter's** (= Peter's books). They're **his** books. They're **his**.

A Read and circle the correct words.

1. Q: Whose bicycle (is)/ are) that?   A: It's (Sandra's / hers) bicycle.

2. Q: Whose jackets (is / are) these?   A: They're (his / him) jackets.

3. Q: Whose house (is / are) that?   A: It's (Tom's / Tom).

4. Q: Whose jeans (is / are) those?   A: They're (our / ours) jeans.

5. Q: Whose teddy bear (is / are) this?   A: It's (Nancy / hers).

6. Q: Whose shopping bags (is / are) those?   A: They're (their / theirs) shopping bags.

A Complete the questions and write short answers, as in the example.

1. skirt / I → Q: _Whose skirt_ is this? A: _It's my skirt._ _It's mine._

2. T-shirt / you → Q: _____ is that? A: _____ _____

3. boots / she → Q: _____ are these? A: _____ _____

4. keys / he → Q: _____ are those? A: _____ _____

5. ball / they → Q: _____ is that? A: _____ _____

B Look and answer the questions.

1.
Peter / bike

Q: Is this Peter's bike?

A: _Yes, it is. It is his bike._

2.
Bill / truck

Q: Is this Bill's truck?

A: _____

3.
Laura / blackboard

Q: Is this Laura's blackboard?

A: _____

4.
Molly & Paul / dog

Q: Is this Molly and Paul's dog?

A: _____

5.
Ann / umbrella

Q: Is this Ann's umbrella?

A: _____

Make questions with *whose*, *that/those* and answer them.

1.

computer? → the children

Q: Whose computer is that?

A: It's the children's.

2.

umbrella? → Paul

Q: _____

A: _____

3.

ice skates? → Alice

Q: _____

A: _____

4.

soccer ball? → the girls

Q: _____

A: _____

 First write and then say as in the example.

	Food	Sport	Singer	Movie Star
William	spaghetti	golf	Rihanna	Megan Fox
Cindy	chicken	swimming	Justin Timberlake	Johnny Depp
Bob & Jane	fish and chips	soccer	Elton John	Angelina Jolie

spaghetti

chicken

fish and chips

1. William's favorite food is spaghetti. His favorite sport is golf. His favorite singer is Rihanna. His favorite movie star is Megan Fox.

2. _____
   _____

3. _____
   _____

4. My favorite food is _____
   _____

A Look at the example and practice with a partner. (Repeat 3 times.)

1.

Is this your wallet?   No, it isn't mine.

Whose is it, then?   I think it's Kevin's. His wallet is black.

1. (wallet)
Kevin / black

2. (shoes)
Jason / brown

3. (hamburger)
Olivia / very big

4. (digital camera)
the children / silver

5. (car)
Sally / very old

B Work with a partner. Ask a question with *Whose.*

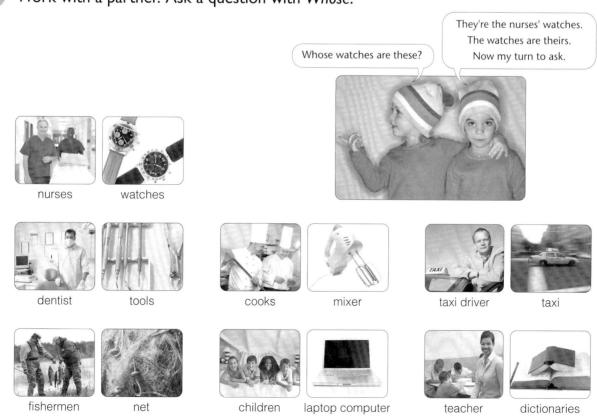

Whose watches are these?

They're the nurses' watches.
The watches are theirs.
Now my turn to ask.

nurses   watches

dentist   tools   cooks   mixer   taxi driver   taxi

fishermen   net   children   laptop computer   teacher   dictionaries

Count/Noncount Nouns, Quantity Questions

Count (or Countable) and Noncount (or Uncountable) Nouns

- 셀 수 없는 명사는 하나, 둘, 셋… 이렇게 수를 셀 수가 없어요. 그래서 명사 앞에 부정관사 a/an을 붙일 수도 없고, 명사 끝에 -s나 -es를 붙여 복수형을 만들 수도 없답니다.

She drinks too much **coffee**.

We need a secretary with **experience**.

How much **water** do you want?

액체	oil(기름), shampoo(샴푸)
고체	gold(금), soap(비누), silver(은), plastic(플라스틱), furniture(가구), clothing(의류)
기체	air(공기), gas(가스, 기체)
음식	food(음식), butter(버터), cheese(치즈), bread(빵), fruit(과일), water(물), juice(주스), coffee(커피), tea(차), soup(수프), milk(우유), rice(쌀), salt(소금), pepper(후추), sugar(설탕)
과목	math(수학), history(역사), English(영어), science(과학), music(음악)
운동 이름	soccer(축구), baseball(야구), basketball(농구), tennis(테니스), golf(골프), volleyball(배구)
눈에 보이진 않지만 이름이 있는 것들	help(도움), work(일), music(음악), advice(충고), information(정보), homework(숙제), happiness(행복), love(사랑), experience(경험)

A Put the words in the right column.

egg　　　ice cream　　　homework　　　salt　　　dress　　　sandwich

Count	Noncount
egg	

Units of Measure with Nouns

- 셀 수 없는 물질 명사는 그 물질을 담는 그릇을 나타내는 말을 이용하여 셀 수 있어요.

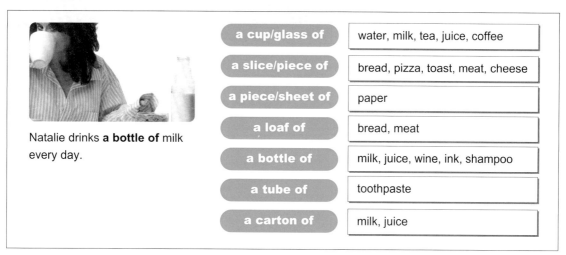

Natalie drinks **a bottle of** milk every day.

a cup/glass of	water, milk, tea, juice, coffee
a slice/piece of	bread, pizza, toast, meat, cheese
a piece/sheet of	paper
a loaf of	bread, meat
a bottle of	milk, juice, wine, ink, shampoo
a tube of	toothpaste
a carton of	milk, juice

E.g. two glass**es** of water, three slice**s** of pizza, four loa**ves** of bread

---

A Fill in the blanks.

1.

a _____tube_____ of toothpaste

2.

three _____ of pizza

A(n), Some, and Any

- a/an은 개수가 '하나, 한 개'로 정해져 있는 단수 명사 앞에 쓰지만, some과 any는 우리가 정확하게 어떤 수나 양을 모를 때 사용하는 말이에요. '몇몇의, 약간(조금)'의 뜻으로, 단수/복수 명사 앞에 모두 쓸 수 있어요.
- some은 주로 긍정문에 쓰고 any는 주로 부정문과 의문문에 씁니다.

A: There is **an** apple. Is there **any** cheese?
B: No, there isn't **any** cheese.
 There isn't **any** cheese, but there is **some** water.

A Complete the sentences with *a(n)*, *some*, or *any*.

1.

There is _____ money in the woman's hand.

2.

There is _____ orange.

3.

Are there _____ books on the bed?

Quantity Questions

- how many와 how much는 '얼마나'의 뜻으로, 그 수와 양을 물어보는 말이에요. how many 뒤에는 셀 수 있는 복수 명사를 쓰고, how much 뒤에는 셀 수 없는 명사를 써서 물어봐요.

Bob: **How many** teaspoons of sugar do you take in your tea?
Susan: I love sugar. I want lots of sugar. Three teaspoons, please.
Bob: And milk? **How much** milk do you want?
Susan: Oh, I don't want much milk. Just a little.

A Fill in the blanks with *how many* or *how much*.

1. ___How many___ books are there in your room?

2. _____ water do you drink?

3. _____ money do you have?

4. _____ sugar does she put in the coffee?

5. _____ apples do they have?

6. _____ cities does Tom visit?

B Underline and correct the mistakes.

1. How much milk <u>are</u> there in the bottle?   →   ___is___

2. How much dresses are there in your wardrobe? → _____

3. How much moneys do you have?   →   _____

4. How many time do you need?   →   _____

A Write questions with *how many* or *how much*, as in the example.

1. coffee / the cup

 → How much coffee is there in the cup? _____

2. Coke / the bottle

 → _____

3. eggs / the fridge

 → _____

4. tea / the cup

 → _____

5. tomatoes / the bag

 → _____

6. soup / the bowl

 → _____

7. strawberry juice / the glass

 → _____

B Look at the picture and complete the sentences.

1. ___Is there any milk on the table___? (milk)

 Yes, _____there is some milk_____.

2. _____? (bread)

 Yes, _____.

3. _____? (onions)

 No, _____.

4. _____? (apples)

 Yes, _____.

5. _____? (rice)

 No, _____.

6. _____? (orange juice)

 Yes, _____.

C Have you got any of the things below? Use a dictionary if necessary. Write some sentences with *some* or *any*.

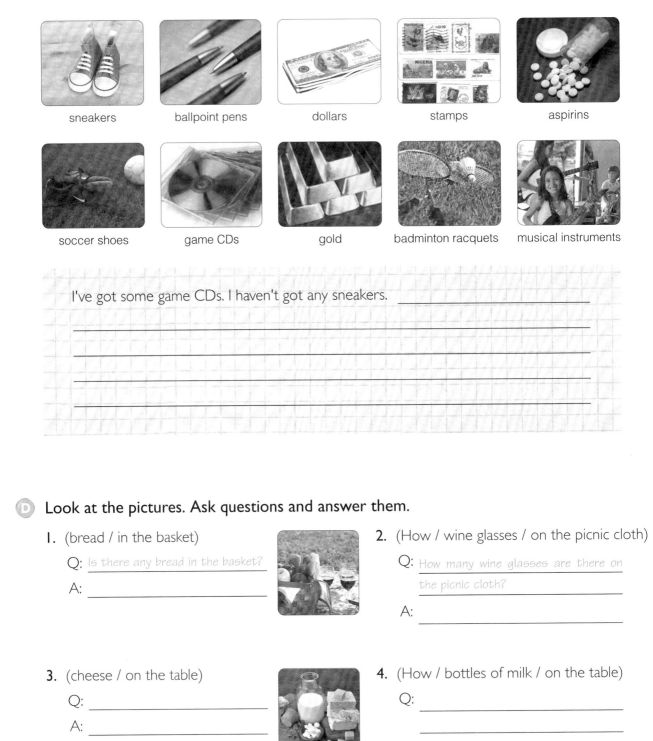

sneakers   ballpoint pens   dollars   stamps   aspirins

soccer shoes   game CDs   gold   badminton racquets   musical instruments

I've got some game CDs. I haven't got any sneakers. _____

_____

_____

_____

_____

D Look at the pictures. Ask questions and answer them.

1. (bread / in the basket)

   Q: Is there any bread in the basket?

   A: _____

2. (How / wine glasses / on the picnic cloth)

   Q: How many wine glasses are there on the picnic cloth?

   A: _____

3. (cheese / on the table)

   Q: _____

   A: _____

4. (How / bottles of milk / on the table)

   Q: _____

   _____

   A: _____

5. (oranges / in the fridge)

   Q: _____

   A: _____

6. (How / juice / in the fridge)

   Q: _____

   _____

   A: _____

A Look at the example and practice with a partner. Use the words below or invent your own. (Repeat 3 times.)

1.

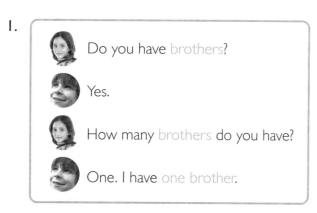

Do you have brothers?

Yes.

How many brothers do you have?

One. I have one brother.

1. brothers? / one brother

2. girlfriends? / three

3. drink milk every day? / two glasses

B Work in pairs. Ask and answer about what you usually eat (or drink) every day. Use the words from the vocabulary box.

How much water do you drink every day?

Eight glasses. (I drink eight glasses of water.)

Your turn to ask!

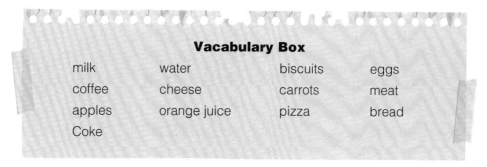

Vacabulary Box

milk	water	biscuits	eggs
coffee	cheese	carrots	meat
apples	orange juice	pizza	bread
Coke			

Unit 10 *Will*, Articles (Definite/Zero)

Unit Focus
- *Will*
- Definite Article: *The*

Will

- will은 앞으로의 일을 예측하거나, 미래의 일에 대해서 순간적으로 결정할 때 써요. '~일 것이다, ~할 것이다'의 뜻으로 will 뒤에는 반드시 동사 원형을 씁니다.

Future Prediction

Scientists **will** find a cure for AIDS one day.

Decision at the Time of Speaking

Those shoes are very comfortable. I **will** buy them.

Future Tense	
Affirmative: *Will*	**Negative: *Will Not* (= *Won't*)**

I/You/We/They He/She/It	**will go** fishing tomorrow.	I/You/We/They He/She/It	**won't go** fishing tomorrow.

- 부정문은 will 뒤에 not만 붙이면 돼요. 일상 영어에서는 주로 주어와 will을 축약해서 사용해요.

I will → I'll   You → You'll   He will → He'll
She will → She'll   They will → They'll   It → It'll

A Circle the correct words and check the boxes.

Future Predictions   Instant Decisions

1. A: We've run out of milk.
   B: Oh, have we? I will (go / goes) and get some.

2. A: My suitcase is very heavy.
   B: I (will carry / will be carry) it for you.

3. A: Nancy eats better food and takes more exercise.
   B: She will (is / be) healthier.

4. A: I've lost a tennis ball.
   B: We (help will / will help) you look for it.

B Use the notes to write about what will happen in the future.

1. it / be / warm / tomorrow → *It will be warm tomorrow.*

2. Olivia's party / be / fun → _____

3. Bob / not watch / the match → _____

4. William / study / all weekend → _____

5. Laura / not do / any work → _____

Will: Yes/No Questions

- will을 이용한 의문문은 will을 문장 맨 앞으로 보내고 물음표(?)만 붙이면 돼요. 대답은 yes나 no를 사용해서 하지요.
- 부정의 대답은 주로 축약형을 쓰지만, 긍정의 대답에서는 주어와 축약해서 쓰지 않아요.

Q: **Will** people live on other planets in the future?
A: **Yes**, they **will**. / **No**, they **won't**.

Q: **Will** Ava go shopping tomorrow?
A: **No**, she **won't**. She will jog.

Questions

Will you jog tomorrow?
Will she visit the zoo?
Will he learn Spanish?
Will they attend the conference tomorrow?
Will it rain tomorrow?

Answers

Yes, I **will**. / No, I **won't**.
Yes, she **will**. / No, she **won't**.
Yes, he **will**. / No, he **won't**.
Yes, they **will**. / No, they **won't**.
Yes, it **will**. / No, it **won't**.

A Make *yes/no* questions and answer them.

1. She will make a sandwich.

   Q: _____*Will she make a sandwich?*_____   A: No, ___*she won't*___ .

2. It will be cold tomorrow.

   Q: _____   A: Yes, _____ .

3. He'll be a third grader next year.

   Q: _____   A: Yes, _____ .

Definite Article: *The*

- 정관사 the는 앞서 언급된 명사가 다시 반복될 때, 또는 말하는 사람이나 듣는 사람이 무엇을 가리키는지 알 수 있는 '특정한 것', '바로 그것'이라는 뜻을 가리킬 때 사용해요.

Jennifer has **a** car. **The** car is black.

A: Look! **The** children are in the house.
B: No, they're outside, in **the** garden.

- 지구나 태양과 같이 세상에서 유일한 것 그리고 악기 앞에는 정관사 the를 써요.

The earth revolves around **the** sun.

She can play **the** flute and **the** piano.

- 과목, 스포츠, 언어, 식사, 도시, 국가를 나타내는 명사 앞에는 정관사 the를 쓰지 않아요.

Q: What do you have for **breakfast**?
A: I drink a glass of orange juice.

Subjects: history, science, math
Sports: soccer, basketball, baseball
Languages: English, Korean, Japanese
Meals: breakfast, lunch, dinner
Cities: Seoul, London, Seattle
Countries: France, Korea, China

A Write *a(n)* or *the* in the blanks. Put an X if you don't need an article.

1. Can you speak ___X___ German?

2. Do you play _____ tennis?

3. He is _____ boy we saw on television.

4. Look at _____ sun.

5. We like _____ Korea.

6. _____ moon is beautiful tonight.

7. She has _____ truck. The truck is old.

8. My favorite sports are _____ soccer and _____ skiing.

A Look at the pictures and complete the sentences. Use *the* if necessary.

1.   2.   3.   4.   5.

1. _____The sun_____ is shining.

2. She is playing _____.

3. He is playing _____.

4. _____ is very clear.

5. Scott doesn't like _____.

B Write questions and complete the short answers.

1. Q: Will you be at home tomorrow night? _____

   A: No, _____I won't_____. (I won't be at home tomorrow night.)

2. Q: _____

   A: Yes, _____. (Jane will meet her family next Christmas.)

3. Q: _____

   A: No, _____. (Jason and Cindy won't be at the party.)

4. Q: _____

   A: Yes, _____. (Jessica will arrive in Seoul next week.)

C Say what your decision is in these situations, or what you offer to do. Use these verbs: *carry, have, post, shut*.

1. You and your friend have come into the room. It's a little cold. The window is open, and it is very cold.

   → I will shut the window. _____

2. The choice on the menu is fish or chicken. You hate fish.

   → _____

3. You are meeting a friend at the airport. She has two suitcases. There's a bag, too.

   → _____

4. Your friend has written a letter. You are going to walk into town past the post office.

   → _____

D Hana is asking a fortune-teller about her future. Write questions and answers. Use the future *will*.

1. I / go / to Seoul National University? → No / Yonsei University

   Q: Will I go to Seoul National University?

   A: No, you won't. You'll go to Yonsei University.

2. I / become / a movie star? → No / a teacher

   Q: _____

   A: _____

3. I / get married? → Yes

   Q: _____

   A: _____

4. my husband and I / have / two children? → No / five

   Q: _____

   A: _____

5. we / live in / Seoul? → No / Busan

   Q: _____

   A: _____

E Fill in *a*, *an*, or *the* where necessary. Put an **X** if you don't need an article.

___X___ Mr. Jones has _____ new office. It has

_____ desk, _____ telephone, and _____

expensive computer. He has _____ secretary.

_____ secretary is on _____ phone now.

Mr. Jones and _____ his secretary are very busy in

_____ office today.

A Look at the example and practice with a partner. Use the words below or invent your own. (Repeat 3 times.)

I.

> Can you clean the car?
>
> Sure, I'll clean it this afternoon.
>
> Do you promise?
>
> Yes, I promise. I'll clean it this afternoon.

I.

clean the car? / this afternoon

2.

call me later? / tonight

3.

fix the car? / tomorrow

B Interview! Talk about the questions below with a partner. Write your answers.

1. What do you think we'll have a cure for cancer?
2. Will the world's population get smaller?
3. Will pollution be much worse?
4. Will people travel around the world by space shuttle?
5. Will people live on the earth even in one hundred years' time?
6. Will people live to be 200 years old?

> What do you think we'll have a cure for cancer?
>
> I don't know. But when people start leading healthier lives, we'll have less cancer.

My partner: _____ (name)

I. I don't know. But when people start leading healthier lives, we'll have less cancer.

2. _____

3. _____

4. _____

5. _____

6. _____

Unit **11** **Simple Past of** *Be*

Unit Focus
- ▶ Affirmatives
- ▶ Negatives
- ▶ Questions

Learn & Practice 1

Simple Past: *Be*

- be 동사의 과거는 was와 were 이렇게 두 가지 형태밖에 없어요. 주어가 한 명(하나)인 단수인 경우에 was를 쓰고 여러 명(여러 개)인 복수인 경우에 were를 써 주면 돼요. 우리말 '~이었다, 있었다'의 뜻이에요.
- 주로 과거를 나타내는 ago, yesterday, last night/year/month/week 등과 자주 쓰여요.

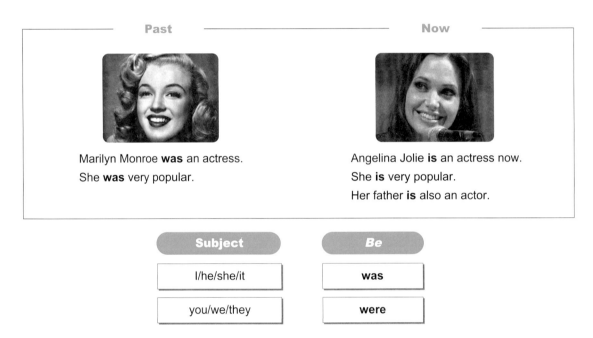

Past	Now
Marilyn Monroe **was** an actress. She **was** very popular.	Angelina Jolie **is** an actress now. She **is** very popular. Her father **is** also an actor.

Subject	Be
I/he/she/it	was
you/we/they	were

A Complete the sentences using *was* or *were*.

1. She _____ very tired yesterday.
2. They _____ very happy together.
3. You _____ very angry with me last night.
4. I _____ in bed all morning.
5. Ruth _____ on holiday last week.
6. Scott and his brother Josh _____ here last night.

B Complete the sentences with *is*, *was*, *are*, or *were*.

1. Fifty years ago, Bert _____ a composer.
2. Dawson _____ born in 1898.
3. Kevin _____ 60 years old today.
4. They _____ with their children today.
5. Kevin and Betty _____ young forty years ago.
6. Kelly _____ at the library all day yesterday.

Past of *Be*: Negatives

- be 동사 과거형의 부정문은 was와 were 바로 뒤에 'not'만 붙이면 돼요. 우리말 '아니었다, 있지 않았다'의 뜻이에요.
- 부정문은 주로 wasn't(=was not), weren't(=were not)처럼 축약형으로 자주 써요.

Yuri Gagarin **wasn't** a police officer.
He **was** an astronaut.

Leonardo da Vinci **wasn't** a doctor.
He **was** a famous painter.

They **weren't** happy.
They **were** angry.

Negative			
Subject	**Be**	**Not**	**Contractions**
I	was		I **weren't**
you	were	not	you **weren't**
he/she/it	was		he/she/it **wasn't**
we/they	were		we/they **weren't**

A Complete the sentences. Use *wasn't* or *weren't*.

1. Susan is here today, but _____*she wasn't here*_____ yesterday.

2. Lucy is busy today, but _____ yesterday.

3. Steve is at the library tonight, but _____ yesterday afternoon.

4. Kathy and Bob are at my house today, but _____ yesterday.

5. You're in sports class this month, but _____ last month.

6. It's cold this week, but _____ last week.

7. Olivia is my classmate this year, but _____ last year.

Past of *Be: Yes/No* Questions

- be 동사의 과거형인 was와 were를 문장 맨 앞으로 보내고 물음표(?)를 써 주면 돼요.
- 의문문에 대한 대답은 현재형과 똑같이 be 동사를 그대로 사용하고 yes나 no로 대답해요. 주어도 알맞은 대명사로 바꿉니다. yes로 짧게 대답하는 경우에는 주어와 be 동사를 줄여서 답하지 않아요.

Q: **Was** Andre Kim a musician?
A: **No**, he **wasn't**. He was a fashion designer.
Q: **Was** he Japanese?
A: **No**, he **wasn't**.
Q: What nationality **was** he?
A: He was Korean.

Questions	Answers	
Was I...?	Yes, you **were**.	No, you **weren't**.
Were you...?	Yes, I **was**.	No, I **wasn't**.
Was he/she/it...?	Yes, he/she/it **was**.	No, he/she/it **wasn't**.
Were we...?	Yes, you **were**.	No, you **weren't**.
Were you...?	Yes, we **were**.	No, we **weren't**.
Were they...?	Yes, they **were**.	No, they **weren't**.

A Write questions and complete the short answers.

1. It was rainy yesterday.
   Q: _____Was it rainy yesterday?_____   A: Yes, ____it was____.

2. She was at home yesterday.
   Q: _____   A: No, _____.

3. Tom was tired last night.
   Q: _____   A: Yes, _____.

4. The movie was great.
   Q: _____   A: No, _____.

5. They were in class yesterday.
   Q: _____   A: Yes, _____.

6. Lisa and I were at the park.
   Q: _____   A: No, _____.

A Use the prompts below to ask and answer questions, as in the example.

1.

Mozart / painter?
→ No / musician

2.

Van Gogh /
from Germany?
→ No / from Holland

3.

Cleopatra / American?
→ No / Egyptian

4.

Alexander Graham Bell /
architect?
→ No / inventor

1. Q: Was Mozart a painter?
   A: No, he wasn't. He was a musician.

2. Q: _____
   A: _____

3. Q: _____
   A: _____

4. Q: _____
   _____
   A: _____

B Complete the story, adding *was* or *were*. Match each text to a photo.

1.
He _____ an actor and fighter. He _____ born on November 27th, 1940 in San Francisco. His parents _____ from Hong Kong. They _____ not rich. His father _____ a singer. His last film _____ *Enter the Dragon.* He _____ short and thin, but he _____ very strong and very fast.

a.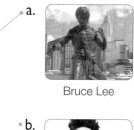

Bruce Lee

b.

Elvis Presley

2.
She _____ a princess and a fashion icon. She was born on July 1st, 1961 in Sandringham. Her parents _____ rich. She _____ not a good student at school, but she _____ a good pianist. Her wedding _____ in St Paul's Cathedral in London. Her husband _____ Prince Charles. Their life together _____ not happy.

c.

Princess Grace

d.

Diana,
Princess of Wales

C Write five sentences about things that happened to you yesterday.

1. I was at the bookstore yesterday. (I was happy yesterday.)

2. _____

3. _____

4. _____

5. _____

6. _____

D Look at the pictures. Use the prompts to make questions and then answer them.

1.

you / at a restaurant / last Saturday?

Q: Were you at a restaurant last Saturday?

A: Yes, we were.

2.

you / in Egypt / last week?

Q: _____

A: _____

3.

Nancy and Peter / in the movie theater / yesterday?

Q: _____

A: _____

4.

they / at the art gallery / last Monday?

Q: _____

A: _____

E Answer these questions about yourself!

1. Where were you born?　　→　_____

2. When was your last birthday?　→　_____

3. Where were you on your birthday?　→　_____

4. How old were you five years ago?　→　_____

A Look at the example and practice with a partner. Use the words below or invent your own. (Repeat 3 times.)

1.

 How **was** the zoo in Seoul?

 It **was** interesting. How **was** the pizza in New York?

 It **was** delicious.

1.
A: How / the zoo in Seoul?
B: interesting / How / the pizza in New York?
A: delicious

2.
A: How / the concert?
B: very crowded / How / the food / in Korea?
A: very delicious

3.
A: How / your vacation?
B: great / How / the weather in Tokyo?
A: a little hot

4.
A: How / the museums in London?
B: boring and crowded / How / the exhibition in Seoul?
A: fantastic

B Work with a partner. Ask and answer questions about the chart as in the example.

Were you at home yesterday? Where were you?

No, I wasn't. I was at a party yesterday.

Place (Questions)	Place (Answers)	Time
at home (x)	at a party (o)	yesterday
at school (x)	at a theater (o)	last night
at the cafe (x)	at the beach (o)	last Saturday
at the park (x)	in class (o)	yesterday afternoon
at the movie theater (x)	at a restaurant (o)	last night
in New York (x)	in London (o)	last summer

* Switch roles.

My partner: _____ (name)

He (or She) was at a party yesterday. _____

_____

_____

_____

_____

Simple Past of *Be* **71**

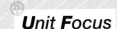

Simple Past: Regular Verbs

- 과거 시제는 이미 지나간 행동이나 상황을 나타내어 현재와는 아무런 관련이 없어요. '~했다, ~했었다'의 뜻으로 해석해요. 주로 동사에 -(e)d를 붙여서 과거형을 만들죠.

- 부정문은 주어의 인칭이나 수와 관계없이 동사 앞에 did not을 쓰고 동사는 원형 그대로 써요. 일상 영어에서는 did not을 didn't로 줄여서 씁니다.

Every weekend I stay at my aunt's house.
But last weekend I **stayed** at my grandmother's house.

I **didn't finish** my homework yesterday.
My teacher is very angry.

Affirmative		**Negative**	
I/We/You He/She/It/They	**watched** TV.	I/We/You He/She/It/They	**didn't watch** TV.

Ⓐ Complete the sentences in the simple past tense.

1. [rain] It __rained__ a lot yesterday evening.

2. [not walk] I _____ to the bus stop.

3. [ask] Yesterday she _____ many questions in science class.

4. [not play] The children _____ basketball last night.

5. [watch] We _____ a DVD yesterday.

6. [not stay] Sunny _____ with me last night.

Simple Past: *Yes/No* Questions

- 의문문은 주어가 무엇이든 관계없이 did를 문장 맨 앞에 쓰고 물음표(?)를 쓰면 돼요. did가 과거임을 나타내기 때문에 주어 뒤에 있는 동사는 반드시 동사 원형을 써야 해요.
- 의문문에 대한 대답은 yes나 no로 하고, 주어와 관계없이 긍정일 때에는 'Yes, 주어 + did.', 부정일 때에는 'No, 주어 + didn't.'로 답하면 돼요.

Did Kathy learn yoga last night?

Yes, she **did**.

No, she **didn't**.

Did	Subject	Base Verb		Answers	
Did	I/we/you he/she/it/they	work? (동사 원형)		**Yes**, I/we/he, etc. **did**	**No**, I/we/he, etc. **didn't**.

Ⓐ Make *yes/no* questions and complete the short answers.

1. Elizabeth graduated last summer.
   Q: _____Did Elizabeth graduate last summer?_____   A: Yes, _____she did_____.

2. They invited six people.
   Q: _____   A: No, _____.

3. The guests arrived on time.
   Q: _____   A: Yes, _____.

4. The fire started in the oven.
   Q: _____   A: No, _____.

5. The shop closed ten minutes ago.
   Q: _____   A: Yes, _____.

6. She walked to school yesterday.
   Q: _____   A: No, _____.

7. He opened the windows.
   Q: _____   A: Yes, _____.

Spelling of Regular Past Verbs

- 과거형은 주어의 단수, 복수와 관계없이 형태가 같아요. 보통 일반 동사 끝에 -ed를 붙여서 과거형을 만들죠. 일정한 규칙으로 모양이 변해요.

대부분의 동사 → 동사 원형에 -ed를 붙임.	show → show**ed** help → help**ed** visit → visit**ed** walk → walk**ed** want → want**ed**
-e로 끝나는 동사 → 동사 원형에 -d를 붙임.	like → like**d** live → live**d** love → love**d** dance → dance**d** move → move**d**
『자음 + -y』로 끝나는 동사 → -y를 -i로 고치고 -ed를 붙임.	stu**dy** → stud**ied** cry → cr**ied** try → tr**ied** worry → worr**ied**
『단모음 + 단자음』으로 끝나는 동사 → 자음을 한 번 더 쓰고 -ed를 붙임.	st**op** → stop**ped** dr**op** → drop**ped** pl**an** → plan**ned**

Ⓐ Write the simple past of these verbs.

1. want → *wanted*

2. walk → _____

3. love → _____

4. try → _____

5. stop → _____

6. drop → _____

7. plan → _____

8. study → _____

9. play → _____

10. help → _____

11. stay → _____

12. live → _____

Ⓑ Rewrite the sentences in the simple past tense.

1. Nancy calls me. → *Nancy called me.*

2. Bob doesn't clean his room. → _____

3. Tiffany works at a bakery. → _____

4. She listens to the customers very carefully. → _____

5. Sam doesn't visit Paris. → _____

A Change the past tense affirmative sentences to negative.

1. Yesterday I asked the teacher a question.

   → *Yesterday I didn't ask the teacher a question.*

2. The government created two million jobs in the last few years.

   →

3. Yesterday she listened to music on the radio.

   →

4. Other nations invested their money in the United States.

   →

5. The country faced serious economic problems.

   →

6. Kevin stayed home in the evening.

   →

B Look and answer the questions.

1.

   listen to / music

   Q: Did Alice watch TV?

   A: *No, she didn't. She listened to music.*

2.

   play / soccer

   Q: Did they play badminton?

   A:

3.

   walk / on the beach

   Q: Did Kelly walk on the street yesterday?

   A:

4.

   stay / at home

   Q: Did Jane and Tom visit a museum?

   A:

C Write sentences about what you did yesterday.

1. Yesterday. I played tennis with my father.

2. _____

3. _____

4. _____

5. _____

6. _____

7. _____

D Look at the pictures and make questions and answers.

1. Rachel / wash / her face?
   → No / wash / her hands

   Q: Did Rachel wash her face?

   A: No, she didn't. She washed her hands.

2. Emma and Henry / watch a movie on television?
   → No / visit / their grandparents

   Q: _____

   A: _____

3. Smith / paint / a picture / two weeks ago?
   → No / paint / a house

   Q: _____

   A: _____

4. the children / study / for the chemistry test / yesterday
   → No / study / for the history test

   Q: _____

   A: _____

A Look at the example and practice with a partner. Use the words below or invent your own. (Repeat 3 times.)

1.

 Yesterday, I played tennis. What did you do?

 I read a book.

1.

A: play tennis   B: read a book

2.

A: cook dinner   B: use a computer

3.

A: talk to Peter   B: wash some clothes

4.

A: study at the library   B: play in a park

B Talk in pairs. Look at what Olivia did and didn't do yesterday. Ask and answer as in the example.

Did Olivia wash the car yesterday?

No, she didn't. She washed the dishes.

	X	O
1. wash	the car	the dishes
2. visit	an art gallery	her grandparents
3. study	Japanese	Chinese
4. watch	a movie on television	a show
5. listen to	music on the radio	English CDs
6. brush	her hair	her teeth
7. play	tennis	badminton

Unit **13** Simple Past 2

Simple Past: Irregular Verbs

- 동사에 -(e)d를 붙이지 않고 자체의 과거 형태를 가지는 동사를 불규칙 동사라고 해요.
- 부정문과 의문문을 만들 때 마찬가지로 동사는 동사 원형을 그대로 써야 해요.

We **went** to Africa last week.
We **saw** a cheetah there.

I **bought** a digital camera yesterday.
I **took** pictures.

- 아래의 불규칙적으로 변화하는 동사들을 반복해서 읽어 보고 자연스럽게 쓸 수 있도록 암기해 보세요.

Base Form	Past Form	Base Form	Past Form
buy	bought	come	came
see	saw	make	made
take	took	eat	ate
drink	drank	sit	sat
feel	felt	get	got
give	gave	go	went
have	had	hear	heard
write	wrote	read	read
sleep	slept	meet	met
find	found	tell	told
fly	flew	speak	spoke

Ⓐ Write the simple past.

1. tell → _____
2. am → _____
3. run → _____

4. meet → _____
5. read → _____
6. sleep → _____

7. fly → _____
8. eat → _____
9. make → _____

10. have → _____
11. drink → _____
12. take → _____

B Write these sentences in the simple past.

1. I see my grandparents every weekend. (last weekend)
   → I saw my grandparents last weekend.

2. They go to the mountains in the summer. (last summer)
   →

3. Julie meets William from school every afternoon. (this afternoon)
   →

4. She eats a lot in the evenings. (last night)
   →

5. We always have a nice time with them. (on holiday)
   →

6. Tom does exercise for half an hour in the morning. (yesterday)
   →

C Choose and complete the sentences about the past.

do   drink   sit   take

1.

They _____ sat on the bench _____.

2.

Martin _____.

3.

The baby _____ yesterday.

4.
She _____.

Simple Past: *WH-* Questions with Action Verbs

- 의문사가 과거 시제와 함께 쓰일 때에는 '의문사 + did + 주어 + 동사 원형…?'으로 나타내요. yes/no로 대답할 수 없고 의문문에 사용된 시제와 같은 시제로 답을 해야 해요.
- 의문사(who/what) 자체가 주어가 되는 경우 '의문사(Who/What) + 동사…?'의 어순으로 씁니다. did를 쓰지 않아요.

Q: **What did** she have?
A: She had a laptop.

Q: **Who invented** the telephone?
A: Alexander Graham Bell invented it.

WH- Word	Did	Subject	Base Verb
What　When Where　Who How　Why What time	did	I/we/you she/he/it/they	동사원형…?

WH- Word as Subject	Past Tense Verb
Who What	**called**? **happened**?

(A) Complete the questions using *who, what, when, where,* or *why.*

1. Q: ___What___ did you have for breakfast?　　A: I had cereal.

2. Q: _____ did you run?　　A: Because I was late.

3. Q: _____ did Alice come?　　A: At six.

4. Q: _____ did Ann and her brother go?　　A: They went to Beijing.

5. Q: _____ built the Great Pyramid?　　A: King Khufu of Egypt.

6. Q: _____ happened?　　A: The plane ran into a terrible thunder storm.

A Look at the pictures and answer the questions.

1.

at the cafeteria

Q: Did you eat lunch at a restaurant?

A: No, I didn't. I ate lunch at the cafeteria.

2.

the library

Q: Did Tom go to the shopping center last night?

A: _____

3.

green tea

Q: Did Alice have a cup of coffee this morning?

A: _____

4.

by bus

Q: Did they come to school on foot yesterday?

A: _____

B Make questions for each answer. Use *who, what, when, where,* or *why.*

1. Q: Where did you go last night?

   A: To the bookstore. (I went to the bookstore last night.)

2. Q: _____

   A: Last week. (Cindy arrived in Seoul last week.)

3. Q: _____

   A: A sandwich. (Kevin ate a sandwich for lunch.)

4. Q: _____

   A: Olivia. (I saw Olivia at the concert.)

5. Q: _____

   A: Because she had to study. (Laura stayed home last night because she had to study.)

C What did Ava do on holiday last week? Look at her pictures and write sentences. Use the phrases in the box.

1.

2.

3.

4.

1. _____She had a picnic._____

2. _____

3. _____

4. _____

see a fireworks display   play beach volleyball
swim in the sea   have a picnic

D Answer the questions about yourself.

1. What did you do last weekend?

_____

2. What time did you get up yesterday?

_____

3. Where did you go on holiday last summer?

_____

4. What time did you go to bed last night?

_____

5. How many DVDs did you watch last week?

_____

6. How did you get to school today?

_____

E Write questions for each answer. Use the underlined words to help you choose the correct question word.

1. _What did you see?_

→ I saw an <u>airplane</u>.

2. _____

→ I saw <u>Tiffany</u>.

3. _____

→ I saw her <u>yesterday morning</u>.

4. _____

→ She looked <u>angry</u>.

5. _____

→ <u>Alexander Fleming</u> discovered penicillin.

6. _____

→ I ran <u>because I was late</u>.

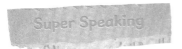

A Look at the example and practice with a partner. Use the words below or invent your own. (Repeat 3 times.)

I.

> Who **did you** meet at the cafe last week?
>
> I **met** my friends.

1.

Who / meet / at the cafe / last week?
→ my friends

2.

Where / go / on vacation?
→ to the beach

3.

How / get to work / yesterday?
→ by subway

B Talk in pairs. Look at the note on Brian's schedule. Ask and answer questions as in the example.

last Saturday

11:00 go shopping with his mother

2:00 go to a baseball game

7:00 watch an English video

three days ago

2:45 practice the piano

6:00 watch a movie on TV

8:00 go to Susan's party

yesterday

2:00 go to the library

4:00 play basketball with Tom

7:00 visit his grandma

What did Brian do at 11:00 last Saturday?

He went shopping with his mother.

Your turn to ask!

Yes, he did.

Did Brian go to a baseball game at 2:00 last Saturday?

Unit 14 Prepositions of Place

Unit Focus
▶ *In, On, At, Under*
▶ *Behind, Between, Next to*
▶ *In Front Of, Near, Across From, Above, Below*

Learn & Practice 1

Prepositions of Place: *In, On, At, Under*

- 전치사는 명사 앞에 착 달라붙어서(전치사 + 명사) 사물이나 사람이 어떤 위치에 있는지를 알려 주는 역할을 해요.
- in(~ 안에)은 건물이나 구체적인 공간 안에 있을 때, on(~ 위에)은 어떤 장소에 접촉하는 표면 위를 말할 때, at(~에)은 정거장, 공항, 영화관과 같이 분명한 장소에 있을 때, under(~ 아래)는 어떤 대상의 아래에 위치했을 때 사용해요.

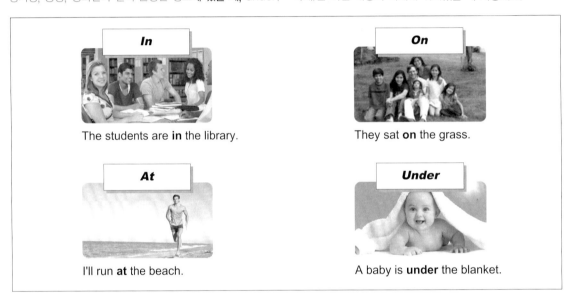

In
The students are **in** the library.

On
They sat **on** the grass.

At
I'll run **at** the beach.

Under
A baby is **under** the blanket.

Ⓐ **Look at the pictures and answer the questions as in the example.**

1.

the wall

Where is the clock?
→ _____ *On the wall.* _____

2.

the airport

Where is he?
→ _____

3.

the tree

Where is she?
→ _____

4.

the box

Where is the girl?
→ _____

Learn & Practice 2

Prepositions of Place: *Behind, Between, Next to*

- behind는 '~의 뒤에', between A and B는 'A와 B 사이에', 그리고 next to는 '~ 옆에'라는 뜻의 전치사예요.
- next to와 by, beside는 서로 뜻이 비슷해요.

Behind

A man is standing **behind** the wall.

Between

Abigail is **between** her mother and father.

Next To

There is a dog **next to** the boy.

By

David is standing **by** the bookcase.

A Where are the people in the picture? Complete the sentences with *behind*, *between*, or *next to*.

1. Alan is standing ___behind___ Donna.

2. Donna is sitting _____ Emma.

3. Emma is sitting _____ Donna and Frank.

4. Colin is standing _____ Frank.

5. Frank is sitting _____ Emma.

6. Barbara is standing _____ Alan and Colin.

A = Alan　　B = Barbara
C = Colin　　D = Donna
E = Emma　　F = Frank

Prepositions of Place: *In Front Of, Near, Across From, Above, Below*

- in front of는 '~ 앞에', near는 '~ 가까이에', across from은 '~의 맞은편에', above는 '(막연한) ~ 위에', 그리고 below는 '(막연한) ~ 아래에'라는 뜻의 전치사예요.

In Front Of

Tom is standing **in front of** the school bus.

Near

I lived **near** the shore last year.

Across From

She sat down **across from** him.

Above / Below

There are pictures **above** the bed.
There is a bed **below** the pictures.

Ⓐ Look at the pictures and answer the questions as in the example.

1.

bed

Q: Where is the picture?

→ _Above the bed._

1.

Eiffel Tower

Q: Where are your parents?

A: _____

3.

building

Q: Where is the man?

→ _____

4.

coast

Q: Where is the boat?

A: _____

A Look at the picture and write the answers.

1. Is the teddy bear behind the chair?

   → _No, it isn't. It is in front of the chair._

2. Where is the lion doll?

   → _____

3. Where is the book?

   → _____

4. Is the apple on the bed?

   → _____

5. Where is the clock?

   → _____

6. Where are the eggs?

   → _____

B Look at the picture. Read and write the answers.

I'm going from New York to Chicago on a train. I'm sitting next to my friend Bob. Two pretty ladies are sitting across from us. My travel bag is in the rack above my head.
Bob has his suitcase under his seat. There's a dining table between our seats and the pretty ladies' seats. There's a cat under the dining table. A ticket inspector is coming down the train. Oh no! Where are our tickets?

1. Where are you sitting? → _I'm sitting next to my friend Bob._

2. Where are the two pretty ladies sitting? → _____

3. Where is your travel bag? → _____

4. Where is Bob's suitcase? → _____

5. Where is the dining table? → _____

6. Where is the cat? → _____

C Look at the picture and correct the sentences.

1. The sofa is above the pictures. → *The sofa is below the pictures.* _____

2. The wardrobe is in front of the window. → _____

3. The mirror is behind the washbasin. → _____

4. The television is under the table. → _____

5. The stereo is on the floor. → _____

6. The pictures are below the sofa. → _____

D Write sentences about the picture. Use the words in brackets.

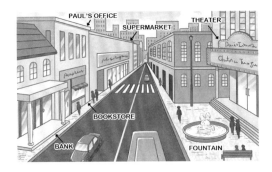

1. (the bank / next to)

   → *The bank is next to the bookstore.* _____

2. (the fountain / in front of)

   → _____

3. (the bookstore / across from)

   → _____

4. (the bookstore / between)

   → _____

5. (Paul's office / near)

   → _____

A Look at the example and practice with a partner. Use the words below or invent your own. (Repeat 3 times.)

1.

Excuse me. I'm looking for Olivia.

She is on the bench.

1. Olivia
2. Tom and Sunny
3. Tommy
4. my brother
5. my puppy
6. Steve

B Work with a partner. Describe the position of the objects using the prepositions given. Your partner must guess the objects.

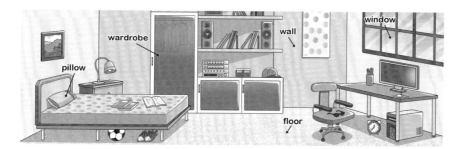

on, under, above, below, next to, in front of, in

It's on the desk and next to the pencils. What is it?

It is the computer monitor.

Your turn to ask!

Unit *Focus*

▶ At, *In, On*
▶ Questions with *When, What Day,* and *What Time*

Prepositions of Time: *At, In, On*

- **at:** 구체적이고 정확한 시각 앞에 써요. at은 한 시점으로 간주되는 때를 나타내요.

| **at** 5 o'clock | **at** lunch (time) | **at** noon | **at** night | **at** midnight |

My mother wakes up **at** 6:00.   I go to school **at** 7 o'clock.   They eat fast food **at** lunch.

- **in:** 달, 계절, 년 등과 같이 비교적 긴 시간 앞에 in을 쓰고 하루의 일부분을 말할 때에도 in을 써요.

| **in** 2014 | **in** (the) spring | **in** August | **in** the morning/afternoon/evening | **in** my free time |

Kathy jogs **in** the morning.

The second semester starts **in** January and finishes **in** May.

- **on:** 날짜, 요일 그리고 하루의 일부분이 아닌 금요일 오후, 일요일 밤과 같은 특정 요일의 일부분에 써요.

| **on** May 15th | **on** Saturday | **on** Friday morning | **on** Christmas day | **on** the weekend (= **on** weekends) |

What do you usually do **on** Saturday?

My birthday is **on** February 5th.

I usually go swimming **on** Tuesdays.

A Read and circle the correct prepositions.

1. What are you doing (**on**/ in) Saturday?

2. Can you wake me up (at / on) 6:00?

3. She goes to the movies (in / on) Saturday evening.

4. The classes start (in / on) September 8th.

5. He was born at 6:00 (at / in) the morning.

6. This street is very quiet (at / on) night.

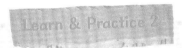
Learn & Practice 2

Questions with *When*, *What Day*, and *What Time*

- when과 what day/time은 시간에 관한 구체적인 정보를 물어볼 때 써요. yes나 no로 대답하지 않고, 시간의 전치사를 이용해서 대답해요.
- what day는 요일에 관련된 on을 쓰고 what time은 구체적인 시간을 나타내는 at을 써서 대답해야 해요.

When is your birthday? ~ It's **on** Sunday.
What day is the party? ~ It's **on** Sunday.
What time is the party? ~ It's **at** 7:00.

Be Verb	Subject	?
When is	your birthday	
What day **What time** is	the party	?

Q: **What time** do you go shopping?
A: I go shopping **at** 6 o'clock.

Q: **When** do you go shopping?
A: I go shopping **at** 6 o'clock.
　　　　　　　on Fridays.
　　　　　　　at noon.
　　　　　　　in the summer.

Helping Verb	Subject	Base Verb
When **What time** do	I/you/we/they	get up?
	does	he/she/it	

A Match the questions with the correct answers.

1. What time does the store open?   •   • a. I eat dinner between 6:00 and 7:00.

2. What day is the concert?   •   • b. I go fishing on Saturdays.

3. What time is the concert?   •   • c. It opens at 9 a.m.

4. When do you go fishing?   •   • d. It's on Monday.

5. When do you eat dinner?   •   • e. It's at 7:00.

B Read the questions. Then, complete the answers with the correct preposition.

1. Q: What time does the post office open?   A: It opens ___at___ 8:30 a.m.

2. Q: When is your English class?   A: It's _____ Monday and Wednesday.

3. Q: What day is the movie   A: It's _____ Friday.

4. Q: When was your mother born?   A: She was born _____ January 1, 1974.

5. Q: When does he go on vacation?   A: He goes on vacation _____ winter.

6. Q: What time do you usually eat breakfast?   A: I eat breakfast _____ 7:30 in the morning.

C Put the words in order to make questions.

1. when / the / supermarket / open? / does   →   *When does the supermarket open?*

2. close? / does / the / what time / bank   →   _____

3. your / is / when / birthday?   →   _____

4. when / visit / do / grandmother? / you / your   →   _____

5. does / your brother / high school? / graduate from / when

     →   _____

A Rewrite the sentences with prepositions of time.

1.

Tom and I went to a shopping mall. (Saturday)

→ Tom and I went to a shopping mall on Saturday.

2.

We have classes. (the morning)

→ _____

_____

3.

School starts. (8 o'clock / the morning)

→ _____

_____

4.

I have my guitar lessons. (10:00 / Wednesdays)

→ _____

_____

B Fill in the blanks with *at*, *in*, or *on*.

1. Goodbye. See you _____ Friday.

Goodbye.

2. Let's meet _____ 8:30 tomorrow morning.

3. When were you born?

_____ 1992.

4. _____ Friday morning, I had a French lesson.

C Read and fill in the blanks with the correct prepositions: *at, in,* or *on.*

My favorite day is Saturday. ___On___ Saturdays I get up _____ 7:00 _____ the morning. I go jogging _____ 8:00, then I eat breakfast. _____ noon I have a sandwich for lunch. After lunch, I watch DVDs or listen to classical music. I usually visit my best friend _____ Saturday afternoon. We watch TV or play badminton. I get home _____ 7 o'clock _____ the evening and have dinner _____ 8:00. After dinner, I sometimes go out with my family. I get back _____ 10:00 and I go to bed _____ 11:00 _____ night. I love Saturdays!

D Read the text in Exercise C again. Which sentences are true? Correct the false ones.

1. Her favorite day is Friday. → Her favorite day is Saturday.

2. She gets up at 7:30 in the morning. → _____

3. After lunch, she goes jogging. → _____

4. She usually visits her best friend on Saturday afternoon.

   → _____

5. She has dinner at 7:00 in the evening. → _____

6. She goes to bed at 11:00 at night. → _____

E Make questions for each answer. Use *when, what day,* or *what time.*

1. Q: When / What time do you have dinner?
   A: I have dinner at 7:00 in the evening.

2. Q: _____
   A: Halloween is on October 31st.

3. Q: _____
   A: I go to bed at around 11:00.

4. Q: _____
   A: Halloween is on Thursday.

5. Q: _____
   A: Christmas is on December 25th.

6. Q: _____
   A: The train leaves at 10:00.

A Look at the example and practice with a partner. Use the words below or invent your own. (Repeat 3 times.)

1.

 What time do you eat breakfast?

 I eat breakfast at 7:00 in the morning.

1.

eat / breakfast?
→ 7:00 / the moring

2.

get up / the morning?
→ seven o'clock / the morning

3.

leave for school?
→ eight o'clock / the morning

4.

do your homework?
→ four o'clock / the afternoon

B Work with a partner. Ask and answer questions with *when*. Use a time expression and *ago* in the answer.

When did you get up?

At seven o'clock, three hours ago.

When did you start learning Korean?

In October, five months ago.

When did you...?
- you get up
- you have breakfast/lunch/dinner
- you get to school
- you take a shower
- you start learning English/Korean/Japanese, etc.
- you learn to ride a bicycle
- your parents get married
- you last eat pizza
- you last see a movie
- you brush your teeth
- you do exercise
- you start at this school
- this term starts
- you last use a smartphone

⊛ **Unit Focus**

▸ Use of Adjectives
▸ Adjective + Noun
▸ *Be* + Adjective

Use of Adjectives

- 형용사는 명사를 꾸며 주는 역할을 하여 명사가 어떻게 생겼는지 어떤 상태나 성질인지를 구체적으로 표현해 주는 말이에요.

She has **long** hair.
She has a **beautiful** smile.
She doesn't like **cold** weather.

You have a **large** house.
Your house is **large**.
The windows are **square**.

| Color |
| red, green, white, yellow, black, blue, etc. |

| Size |
| big, small, tall, short, long, etc. |

Feeling	Shape	Look	Number
happy, sad, angry, nice, good, tired, etc.	round, square, etc.	beautiful, pretty, cute, ugly, old, young, fat, slim, thin, etc.	one, two, three, four, five...

Ⓐ **Look and rewrite the sentences. Use the words in brackers.**

1.  She has eyes. (beautiful)
   → _____She has beautiful eyes._____

2.  That is a table. (round)
   → _____

3.  Tom is a businessman. (nice)
   → _____

4.  It is a lemon. (yellow)
   → _____

Adjective + Noun

- 형용사는 명사 앞에서 명사를 구체적으로 설명해 주는 역할을 해요. 이때 형용사는 명사의 단수, 복수에 관계없이 그 모양이 변하지 않습니다.
- 명사가 다른 명사를 꾸며 주는 형용사 역할을 할 때가 있어요. 명사가 뒤에 있는 다른 명사를 꾸며 주어 하나의 표현이 만들어진답니다.

She is a **pretty** girl.

It is a **cute** puppy.

Luke is holding a **coffee** cup.

I play on the **baseball** team at school.

A Complete the sentences with the adjectives and nouns in brackets.

1. (small / rooms) → They _____*are small rooms*_____ .

2. (not / long / story / a) → It _____ .

3. (happy / children) → They _____ .

4. (quiet / village / a) → It _____ .

5. (heavy / books) → They _____ .

B Tell whether each underlined word is a *noun* or an *adjective*.

1. <u>Women</u> once played professional baseball in a league. → ___*noun*___

2. <u>Women</u> players helped keep baseball alive during World War II. → _____

3. The <u>first</u> toothbrush was invented in 1770. → _____

4. It is important to be a <u>team</u> player. → _____

5. Our <u>team</u> got ready for the game by stretching. → _____

Be + Adjective

- 형용사는 be 동사 뒤에서 주어를 구체적으로 설명해 주는 역할을 하기도 해요. 연결 동사(linking verb)인 be 동사 외에도 seem, look(~처럼 보이다), smell(~처럼 냄새나다), feel(~처럼 느끼다), taste(~처럼 맛이 나다), sound(~처럼 들리다)와 같은 연결 동사 뒤에도 형용사를 써요.
- 국적을 나타내는 형용사는 명사와 모양이 다릅니다. 자주 쓰는 표현은 암기해 두세요.

She is **Canadian**. She is from Canada.
She looks **tired**. She is **unhappy**.

Country	Adjective	Country	Adjective
Italy	Italian	Australia	Australian
Korea	Korean	Brazil	Brazilian
Japan	Japanese	Canada	Canadian
France	French	China	Chinese
Germany	German	England	English
the USA	American	Russia	Russian
Egypt	Egyptian	Portugal	Portuguese

A Rewrite the sentences so that the adjectives come after the verb *be*.

1. She is a pretty girl. → *The girl is pretty.*

2. They are happy girls. → _____

3. They are hungry monkeys. → _____

4. It is a long ruler. → _____

B Complete the sentences as in the example.

1. He is from Korea. He is ___Korean___.

2. She is from Australia. She is _____.

3. We are from Japan. We are _____.

4. I am from Brazil. I am _____.

5. They are from Germany. They are _____.

6. He is from Russia. He is _____.

A Brian is at the mall with his family. Read the sentences. Rewrite the sentences so that the adjectives come before the noun.

1. The bookstore is crowded.　→　It _____is a crowded bookstore_____ .

2. The jewelry store is expensive.　→　It _____ .

3. The music store is noisy.　→　It _____ .

4. The salespeople are kind.　→　They _____ .

5. The children are happy.　→　They _____ .

6. The restaurant is clean.　→　It _____ .

7. The waitress is beautiful.　→　She _____ .

8. The waiter is old.　→　He _____ .

B Look at the picture of Lisa. Write sentences using *is/isn't* and the adjectives in brackets.

Name: Lisa
Nationality: Italian
Marital Status: single
Job: university student
Look: pretty
Height: 173 cm

1. (Egyptian / Italian)　→　_Lisa isn't Egyptian. She is Italian._

2. (single / married)　→　_____

3. (ugly / pretty)　→　_____

4. (short / tall)　→　_____

5. (slim / fat)　→　_____

C Look at the pictures and make sentences as in the example.

1.

his dog / chew up
his shoes

look

→ He looks angry because his dog chewed up his shoes.

2.

get an A+ on the
English test

seem

→ _____

3.

lose her dog

look

→ _____

4.

run a marathon

seem

→ _____

D Complete the sentences with the nouns from the box.

| rope | walking | car | wedding |

1.

This key is used to start the car. It is my _____ car key _____.

2.

The bridge is made of rope. It is a _____.

3.

The shoes are for walking. They are _____.

4.

She bought a dress for her wedding. It is her _____.

A Look at the example and practice with a partner. Use the words below or invent your own. (Repeat 3 times.)

1.

Is it hot food?

No, it isn't. It is cold food.

1.
hot / food?
→ No / cold

2.
sad / students?
→ No / happy

3.
fat / woman?
→ No / thin

4.
light / suitcase?
→ No / heavy

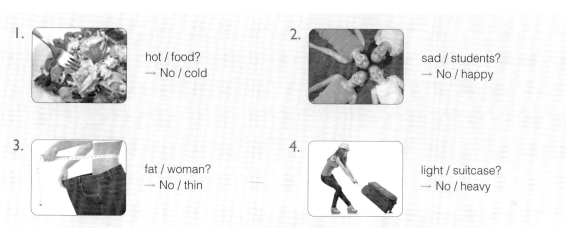

B Work with a partner. Make two sentences for each picture using the words given.

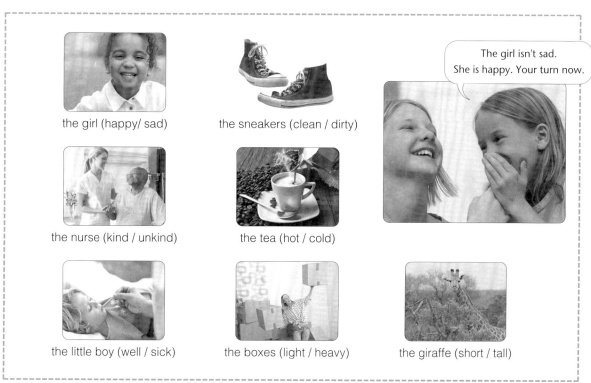

the girl (happy/ sad)

the sneakers (clean / dirty)

The girl isn't sad.
She is happy. Your turn now.

the nurse (kind / unkind)

the tea (hot / cold)

the little boy (well / sick)

the boxes (light / heavy)

the giraffe (short / tall)

Unit 17 Adverbs

Unit Focus
- ▶ Meaning & Uses of Adverbs
- ▶ Rules to Form Adverbs
- ▶ Adverbs of Frequency

Learn & Practice 1

Meaning & Uses of Adverbs

- 부사는 동사, 형용사 또는 다른 부사를 꾸며 주어 그 의미를 더욱 풍부하게 해 주는 역할을 해요.
- 주로 구체적으로 꾸며 주는 말 앞에 쓰고, 동사를 꾸며 줄 때에는 주로 동사 뒤나 문장 맨 뒤에 써요.
- 부사는 주로 어떻게(how), 언제(when), 어디에서(where)에 대한 대답을 나타내죠.

─── Modifying Verbs ───	─── Modifying Adjectives ───	─── Modifying Adverbs ───
The trutle walks **slowly**.	She is **very** beautiful.	He swims **quite** well.
How	*Where*	*When*
Susan lives **happily** with her son.	Steve is **here**.	Farmers wake up **early**.
(**How** does she live? ~ Happily.)	(**Where** is Steve? ~ Here.)	(**When** do farmers wake up? ~ Early.)

Ⓐ Circle the adverbs in each sentence and underline the words they modify.

1. The boys walked quickly.

2. It looks very nice.

3. They arrived early.

4. They started the race slowly.

5. I'm really nervous.

6. In April it often rains heavily.

Ⓑ Underline the adverbs and check *how, when,* or *where.*

	How	When	Where
1. She is dancing beautifully.	√		
2. They are playing outside.			
3. I'm sleepy. I went to bed late last night.			
4. My family lives here.			

Rules to Form Adverbs

- 부사는 보통 형용사에 -ly를 붙여서 만들어요.

Rules of Adverbs	Adjectives	Adverbs
보통 형용사에 -ly를 붙여서 부사를 만들어요.	slow quick beautiful bad loud slow	slow**ly** quick**ly** beautiful**ly** bad**ly** loud**ly** slow**ly**
형용사의 끝이 -y로 끝날 때에는 -y를 -i로 고치고 -ly를 붙여요.	happy easy noisy heavy	happ**ily** eas**ily** nois**ily** heav**ily**
형용사와 부사의 모양이 같은 것들도 있어요.	hard fast late early	**hard** **fast** **late** **early**
형용사와 부사의 모양이 전혀 다른 것도 있어요.	good	**well**

It's an easy language.
You can learn this language **easily**.

Kelly looked hungry.
She ate **hungrily**.

Jane is a good singer.
She sings **well**.

A Write the adverbs of the adjectives below.

1. happy → *happily*

2. quick → _____

3. easy → _____

4. slow → _____

5. careful → _____

6. hard → _____

7. fast → _____

8. good → _____

9. safe → _____

10. bad → _____

11. angry → _____

12. late → _____

Adverbs of Frequency

- 빈도 부사는 어떤 일이 발생하는 횟수, 빈도를 나타내는 부사를 말해요.

- 빈도 부사의 위치는 동사가 일반 동사일 때에는 앞, be 동사(조동사)일 때에는 뒤에 쓰자는 약속이 되어 있어요.

▨▨▨▨▨	always 100%	She is **always** happy.
▨▨▨▨	usually 75%	They **usually** go to the library.
▨▨▨	often 50%	She **often** goes to the zoo.
▨▨	sometimes 25%	My dad **sometimes** plays computer games.
	never 0%	She is **never** late.

- How often 또는 What time (When)에 대한 대답으로 빈도 부사를 자주 써요.

Q: **How often** do you eat vegetables?
A: I **often** eat vegetables.

Q: **What time (When)** do they have breakfast?
A: They **usually** have breakfast at 7:00.

Ⓐ Add the adverb of frequency to each sentence.

1. Kelly is on time. (always) → <u>Kelly is always on time.</u>

2. My mom cooks breakfast. (sometimes) → _____

3. Kelly comes to work on time. (always) → _____

4. We eat hamburgers. (never) → _____

5. He is at work on Sundays. (often) → _____

Ⓑ Complete the questions with *how often*.

1. <u>How often do</u> you eat sandwiches?

2. _____ she brush her teeth?

3. _____ they go to the library?

4. _____ he go on vacation?

5. _____ Bob walk to school?

6. _____ you get up late?

A Look and complete the sentences with *always*, *never*, *usually*, or *sometimes*.

1.

take the school bus

2.

go to the zoo

3.

go shopping on Sunday

4.
wash clothes by hand

1. Tiffany _____ always takes the school bus _____. (100%)

2. Nancy _____. (about 50%)

3. They _____. (about 25%)

4. My mother _____. (0%)

B Read about Ava. Then answer the questions.

Ava is a very careful person. She goes to work on time. She sometimes takes a subway. She works hard at home and at work. She drives her car very carefully. She doesn't drive very fast, and she stops at all the red lights. But, on her way home yesterday evening, she drove badly and almost had an accident.

1. What kind of person is Ava?
   → She is a very careful person.

2. Does she work hard?
   → _____

3. How does she usually drive?
   → _____

4. How often does she take a subway?
   → _____

5. How did she drive yesterday evening?
   → _____

6. Did she have an accident?
   → _____

C Fill in the blanks with the adverbs from the underlined adjective.

1. She's a careful driver. She drives ___carefully___ .

2. She has a beautiful voice. She sings _____ .

3. He is fluent in Korean. He speaks Korean _____ .

4. I'm not a good swimmer. I don't swim _____ .

5. Nurses are hard workers. They work _____ .

6. She looks sad. She said goodbye _____ .

D What does Jason *usually* do in the evening? Look at the pictures and write a sentence to describe each one.

1.

do his homework / 6:00

→ Jason usually does his homework at 6:00 in the evening.

2.

have dinner / 7:00

→ _____

_____

3.

watch TV / 8:00

→ _____

_____

4.

go to bed / 9:00

→ _____

_____

E Write about something you *always* do, something you *usually* do, something you *sometimes* do, and something you *never* do in your daily life. Use the phrases in the box or invent your own.

get up   drink milk   exercise   early/late   go to school   do homework   go to bed

1. I always go to bed early. _____

2. _____

3. _____

4. _____

5. _____

6. _____

A Look at the example and practice with a partner. Use the words below or invent your own. (Repeat 3 times.)

1.

Kathy / watch TV / late at night?
→ never

1.

How often does Kathy watch TV late at night?

She never watches TV late at night.

2.

Nancy / jog / in the morning?
→ always

3.

they / take the school bus?
→ usually

4.

you / take pictures of friends?
→ often

B Interview! Work with a partner. Make questions using the phrases in brackets. Ask and answer them with a partner Then share the information with your class.

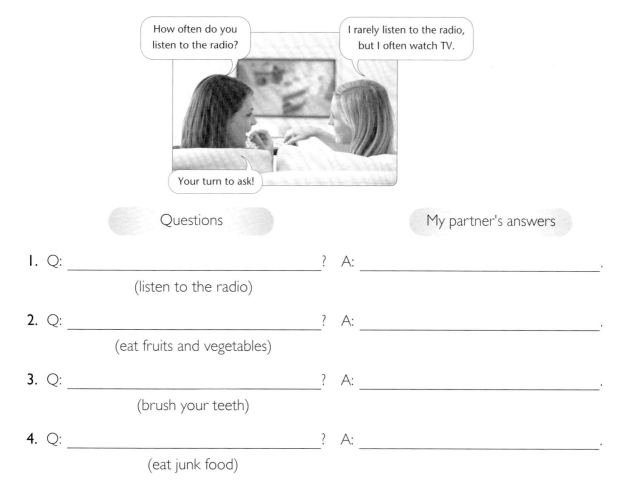

How often do you listen to the radio?

I rarely listen to the radio, but I often watch TV.

Your turn to ask!

Questions

My partner's answers

1. Q: _____ ? A: _____ .
   (listen to the radio)

2. Q: _____ ? A: _____ .
   (eat fruits and vegetables)

3. Q: _____ ? A: _____ .
   (brush your teeth)

4. Q: _____ ? A: _____ .
   (eat junk food)

Unit  **Helping Verbs**

- ▶ *Can/Could* - Ability
- ▶ *May* - Possibility
- ▶ *May, Can*

Learn & Practice

Can/Could – Ability

- can은 '~할 수 있다'의 의미로 현재나 미래의 능력을 나타내고, could는 '~할 수 있었다'의 의미로 과거의 능력을 나타 내요. 조동사 뒤에는 항상 동사 원형만 써야 해요.
- 부정문은 조동사 바로 뒤에 not을 붙이고, 의문문은 조동사를 문장 맨 앞에 쓰고 물음표(?)를 붙여요. 대답은 yes나 no로 하고 의문문에 사용한 조동사를 그대로 사용해서 대답합니다.
- 일상 영어에서 cannot과 could not은 각각 can't, couldn't로 축약형을 써요.

I **can't** swim, so I'm afraid of the water.

My dog is amazing. It **can** sing.

I **could** play the violin last year, but I **can't** play the violin now.

Questions			
Can	I/we/you he/she/it/they	swim	...?
Could	I/we/you he/she/it/they		...?

Answers		
Yes, No,	I/we/you he/she/it/they	can. can't.
Yes, No,	I/we/you he/she/it/they	could. couldn't.

Can you speak Spanish? ~ Yes, I **can**.
~ No, I **can't**.

Could Jane play the piano when she was four?
~ Yes, she **could**. / No, she **couldn't**.

Ⓐ Complete the sentences with *can* or *can't* and the verbs in brackets.

1. Kangaroos ___can jump___ (jump) high, but they ___can't climb___ (climb) trees.

2. Children _____ (drive) a car, but they _____ (ride) a bicycle.

3. A turtle _____ (walk), but it _____ (run).

4. Horses _____ (sleep) when they stand up, but they _____ (live) more than 100 years.

B Make *yes/no* questions and complete the short answers.

1. Yuri can speak English.   Q: _____Can Yuri speak English?_____   A: Yes, _____she can_____ .

2. They could go on a picnic.   Q: _____   A: No, _____ .

3. Tom can finish his homework. Q: _____   A: No, _____ .

4. Sunny and Bob could dance.   Q: _____   A: Yes, _____ .

May – Possibility

- 조동사 may는 '~일지도 모른다'의 뜻으로 가능성이나 확신을 나타내요.
- may는 가능성이 현저히 낮을 때(50% 이하) 쓰고, 어느 정도 가능성이 있다고 판단이 될 때에는 will 또는 현재 진행형을 써서 나타내요.

Tom **may** go to Thailand next year. (It's possible.)

He **will** go to Thailand next year. (It's certain.)

He **isn't going** to Thailand next year. (We know that he won't go.)

Subject	May	Base Verb
I/We/You He/She/It They/Tom, etc.	**may** / **may not**	arrive late.

A Rewrite the sentences as in the examples.

1. It rains tomorrow.   (It's possible.) → _____It may rain tomorrow._____

2. She goes to the interview.   (It's certain.) → _____She will go to the interview._____

3. He goes to the duty-free shop. (It's possible.) → _____

4. I show you the family photos. (It's certain.) → _____

5. The sun rises tomorrow morning. (It's certain.) → _____

6. This street is dangerous at night. (It's possible.) → _____

May, Can

- may와 can은 '~해도 좋다'의 의미로 허락(give permission)을 나타내요. 허락을 나타낼 때 may와 can은 같은 뜻입니다. may not과 cannot은 허락의 부정(refuse permission)으로 '~해서는 안 된다'라는 뜻이에요.
- 상대방에게 정중하게 부탁이나 허락을 요구할 때 May I...? 또는 Can I...?를 써요. 허락을 나타낼 때 can은 가족이나 친구와 같이 편안한 사이에서 쓰고, may는 잘 모르거나 처음 만난 사람 또는 윗사람에게 정중한 표현으로 써요.

You **can't** go out alone at night.

May I see your tickets?
~ Yes, of course.

Can I watch TV tonight, Dad?
~ Okay.

- May I, Can I에 대한 긍정의 대답은 Yes, Yes, of course, Of course, Certainly, Sure, No problem, Okay. 등을 쓰고, 부정의 대답은 I'm sorry, but... 또는 No, I'm sorry. 뒤에 이유를 말해요. No라고만 대답하면 어색하고 무례하다고 생각을 하죠.

A Fill in *can* or *may*.

1. ___May___ I use your phone?
(They don't know each other.)

2. _____ I use your cell phone?
(They are friends.)

3. _____ I ask you a question?
(The teacher is older than me.)

B Read the underlined words and write *possibility*, *ability*, or *permission*.

1. I can find many ways to save money. → ability
2. You may pass the course. → _____
3. May I see your driver's license? → _____
4. They may want a new kind of cereal. → _____
5. You can use my car if you want to. → _____
6. Can Alice remember your phone number? → _____

A Look at the pictures. Write sentences as in the example.

Now
1. (Ava / drive a car)
2. (Susan / cook spaghetti)
3. (Tom / read a newspaper)
4. (John / play water polo)

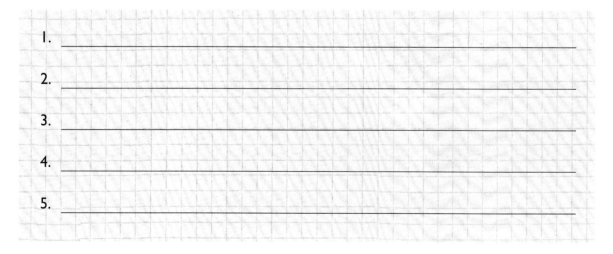

Past
1. (ride a bicycle)
2. (make sandwiches)
3. (draw pictures)
4. (play basketball)

1. Ava can drive a car now. When she was younger, she could only ride a bicycle.

2. _____

3. _____

4. _____

B What can you do? What could you do when you were younger? Write five sentences about yourself.

1. _____

2. _____

3. _____

4. _____

5. _____

C Complete the sentences with *may* as in the example.

1.

have / an accident

→ Laura doesn't drive carefully, so

she may have an accident .

2.

sell / his laptop

→ William needs some money, so

_____ .

3.

become / a fashion designer

→ Kathy likes making clothes, so

_____ .

4.

go / to the stadium

→ Tom and Jim's favorite cheerleader team is in town, so _____

_____ .

D Read the situations below and write sentences making requests.

1. You want to use the phone in your boss's office. What do you say to him?

   → *May I use your phone, please?*
   _____

2. You want to borrow your friend's calculator. What do you say?

   →
   _____

3. Your teacher has a dictionary. You want to borrow it. What do you say?

   →
   _____

4. A friend of yours has been sick in bed for a week. Offer to bring her some comic books to read.

   →
   _____

5. You are at a restaurant. You want to have the check. What do you say to a waiter?

   →
   _____

6. You are at a friend's house. You want to use the telephone. What do you say?

   →
   _____

A Look at the example and practice with a partner. Use the words below or invent your own. (Repeat 3 times.)

1.

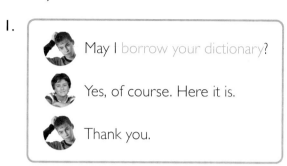

May I borrow your dictionary?

Yes, of course. Here it is.

Thank you.

1. borrow / your dictionary

2. use / your laptop

3. borrow / your pencil

4. have / a glass of water

5. have / the check

B Interview! Work with a partner. Make questions and talk about them.

1. women / be soldiers?

2. a woman / work as a firefighter?

3. a man / be a good nurse?

4. men / work as housekeepers?

5. a woman / be the President of your country?

6. a man / work as a babysitter?

Can women be soldiers?

Yes, they can. There are many women soldiers all over the world.

Your turn to ask!

Helping Verbs **113**

⊛ **Unit Focus**
▶ Imperatives
▶ Suggestion: *Let's*

Imperatives

- 상대방에게 '~해라'라고 명령, 지시, 부탁할 때 주어 You를 쓰지 않고 동사 원형으로 문장을 시작해요. be 동사 am, is, are의 원형은 be예요.
- '~하지 마라'라는 부정의 명령을 나타낼 수도 있어요. 모든 동사 앞에 Don't만 붙여 주면 돼요. 일반 동사든 be 동사든 모두 앞에 Don't를 붙여서 부정 명령문을 나타내요.

To Give Instructions

Use a moderate oven and bake for 20 minutes.

Open your book.

To Give Advice

Don't eat heavy meals.

Go to the dentist.

To Give Orders or Tell People What To do

Do not walk on the grass.

Be quiet in class.

Don't be late for school.

- always, never를 명령문 앞에 써서 상대방을 격려하기도 하는데, never는 또 강한 부정을 나타내기도 해요.
- 부탁이나 요청을 하기 위해 please를 문장 앞이나 뒤에 쓸 수 있지만, 명령문은 윗사람이 아랫사람에게 그리고 상사나 선생님이 부하나 학생들에게 쓰는 표현이므로 주의해야 해요.

To Give Encouragement

Always do your best.

Never swim here.

To Make Requests

Please be quiet. I'm working.

A Make the sentences negative.

1. Please lose weight. → <u>Please don't lose weight.</u>

2. Please wait for me. → _____

3. Read this magazine tonight. → _____

4. Go out for dinner, please. → _____

5. Wash your hands. → _____

B Look and complete the sentences. Use an imperative form of the verbs in the box.

cross   turn   enter   hunt   use   write   smoke   park   pick

1.

<u>Turn</u> left.

2.

_____ flowers.

3.

_____ the road at the lights.

4.

_____ your name here.

5.

_____ your car here.

6.

_____ this road.

7.

Please _____ in this building.

8.

_____ wild animals in the area.

9.

_____ your cell phone.

Let's

- 동사 원형 앞에 Let's를 써서 '(우리 함께) ~하자'라는 뜻의 제안문을 만들 수 있어요. 제안문은 말하는 사람을 포함해 상대방과 주변 사람들에게 제안을 하는 말이에요. Let's는 'Let + us'의 줄임말이에요.
- '~하지 말자'라는 부정문을 쓸 때에는 Let's 바로 뒤에 not만 쓰면 돼요.

Let's + *Base Verb*	*Let's* + *Not* + *Base Verb*

A: It's beautiful day today. What should we do? B: **Let's** go to an amusement park.	A: I'm tired. B: I'm tired, too. **Let's not** go shopping.

A Read and circle the correct words.

1. It's cold outside. (**Let's** / Let's not) go into the house.

2. It's too noisy here. (Let's / Let's not) go to the library.

3. This baseball game is boring. (Let's / Let's not) go play soccer.

4. I am too tired. (Let's / Let's not) go to the movie theater tonight.

5. I'm hungry. There's some bread and cheese. (Let's / Let's not) make sandwiches.

B Read and match. Then write *let's* or *don't*.

1. I'm hungry.   • a. _____ go to the zoo.

2. It's very hot.   • b. _____ talk, please.

3. It's our birthday.   • c. _Let's_ have dinner.

4. I want to see the giraffes.   • d. _____ wear your coat.

5. Shh! I'm watching the movie.   • e. Go to sleep. _____ get up.

6. It's five o'clock in the morning.   • f. _____ open our presents.

A Complete the blanks with an affirmative or a negative imperative.

1.

Nobody is watching TV.

_____Turn off_____ the TV. (turn off)

2.

You are overweight.

_____ the hamburger. (eat)

3.

You're in a public place.

_____ here. (smoke)

4.

You're in the museum.

_____ in the hallway. (run)

5.

Your roommate is listening to music.
It's very loud.

_____ the volume. (turn down)

6.

It's raining now.

_____ an umbrella. (take)

B Look at the pictures and make sentences with *let's* or *let's not*.

1.

make dinner (X)

→ _____Let's not make dinner._____

2.

play basketball (O)

→ _____

3.

swim here (X)

→ _____

4.

go to see a doctor (O)

→ _____

C Your friend wants to lose weight. What do you say to her/him? Look at the pictures and make sentences.

1.

1. Don't eat food at night.

2. _____

_____

3. _____

4. _____

2.

3.

4

D Read and rewrite the sentences with let's.

1. Why don't we go for a picnic? → Let's go for a picnic.

2. Why don't we go to Linda's house-warming party?

→ _____

3. How about going swimming? → _____

4. What about watching TV? → _____

5. Why don't we have lunch at that French restaurant?

→ _____

E Answer with No, don't or No, let's not.

1. Shall I sleep late? → No, don't sleep late.

2. Should we take a taxi? → No, let's not take a taxi.

3. Shall we order pizza for dinner? → _____

4. Shall I wait for you? → _____

5. Should I paint the door? → _____

6. Should I call you tonight? → _____

7. Should we go to school now? → _____

8. Shall I close the window? → _____

A Look at the example and practice with a partner. Use the words below or invent your own. (Repeat 3 times.)

I.

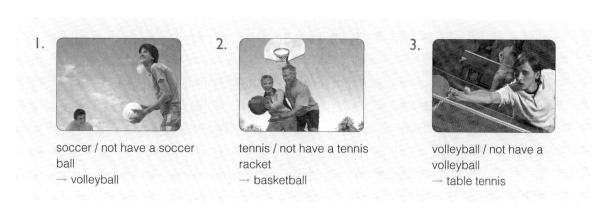

Let's play soccer.

Well, let's play volleyball.

I don't have a soccer ball.

That sounds good.

1.

soccer / not have a soccer ball
→ volleyball

2.

tennis / not have a tennis racket
→ basketball

3.

volleyball / not have a volleyball
→ table tennis

B Work with a partner. Listen to your partner's questions. Make some typical imperative sentences for these situations.

I have a cold. I want to close the window. What do you say to me?

Close the window.
Wear your coat.
Take a hot bath and relax.

Your turn now!

1. I'm trying to study. My roommate is listening to the radio. It's very loud. What do you say to her/him?

2. I have a little sister. She wants to lose weight. She's eating some junk food. What do you say to her?

3. I have a headache with cough and fever. What do you say to me?

4. I have a brother. He's going on vacation to the beach. What do you say to him?

5. I'm worried that I can't speak English very well. What do you say to me?

Unit 20 Questions: the Verb *Be*

Unit Focus
- ▶ *Yes/No* Questions
- ▶ Information Questions with the Verb *Be*

Learn & Practice 1

Yes/No Questions: The Verb *Be* (Present, Past)

- be 동사의 의문문은 be 동사를 문장 맨 앞으로 보내고 물음표(?)를 써 주면 돼요. '~이니?, 있니?'라고 물어보는 말이에요.

- be 동사의 과거형 의문문은 주어가 단수일 때에는 was, 복수일 때에는 were를 문장 맨 앞에 쓰고 물음표(?)를 써요. '~(이)었니?, 있었니?'라는 뜻이에요.

- 대답은 yes나 no로 답하고, 주어는 알맞은 대명사로 바꾸어 대답해야 해요. 부정의 대답은 축약하지만 긍정의 대답은 축약형을 쓰지 않아요.

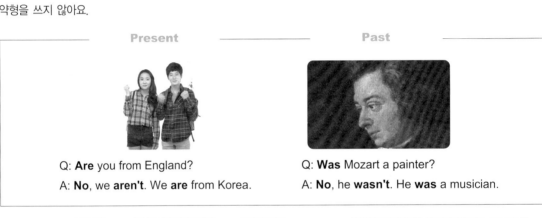

Present	Past
Q: **Are** you from England?	Q: **Was** Mozart a painter?
A: **No**, we **aren't**. We **are** from Korea.	A: **No**, he **wasn't**. He **was** a musician.

Be	Subject	...?	Short Answers	
Am	I		Yes, I am.	No, I'm not.
was			Yes, I was.	No, I wasn't.
Is	he/she/it	tired?	Yes, he is.	No, he isn't.
Was			Yes, she was.	No, she wasn't.
Are	you/we/they		Yes, they are.	No, they aren't.
Were			Yes, we were.	No, we weren't.

(A) Change the sentences to *yes/no* questions.

1. You were tired last night. → *Were you tired last night?*

2. Sunny is at home. → _____

3. He was a teacher ten years ago. → _____

B Choose the correct words and complete each answer.

1. Q: (Are / Is) it an alligator? A: Yes, _____ it is _____.

2. Q: (Are / Am) I late for the class? A: No, _____.

3. Q: (Is / Was) she an elementary school student last year? A: Yes, _____.

4. Q: (Are / Were) Kevin and Jim happy yesterday? A: No, _____.

5. Q: (Was / Is) he at the park now? A: Yes, _____.

Information Questions with the Verb *Be*

- 의문사가 있는 의문문의 어순은 '의문사 + be 동사 + 주어…?'로 써요. 의문사를 이용해 궁금한 것을 자세히 물어보기 때문에 yes나 no로 대답할 수 없어요.
- 궁금한 것이 사람이면 who, 사물이면 what, 장소일 땐 where, 시간이나 날짜는 when, 원인일 땐 why, 사람의 감정이나 상태를 물을 땐 how를 써요.

Q: **What** is it?
A: It is a book.

Q: **How** is she?
A: She is happy.

Q: **Where** were they yesterday?
A: They were at the park.

Q: **Why** was he angry?
A: I have no idea.

- 사람의 직업을 물을 때에도 What is she/he?, What are they?로 물어봐요. 대답은 She is a doctor.처럼 직업을 말하면 되요.

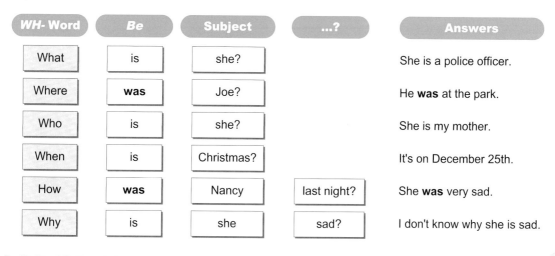

WH- Word	Be	Subject	...?	Answers
What	is	she?		She is a police officer.
Where	**was**	Joe?		He **was** at the park.
Who	is	she?		She is my mother.
When	is	Christmas?		It's on December 25th.
How	**was**	Nancy	last night?	She **was** very sad.
Why	is	she	sad?	I don't know why she is sad.

A Make questions with *be*.

1. Where / John?

   → Where is John?

2. Where / John / yesterday?

   → Where was John yesterday?

3. Why / they / hungry?

   → _____

4. How / the food?

   → _____

5. When / the concert?

   → _____

6. Why / you / late / yesterday?

   → _____

7. How / she / last night?

   → _____

8. Why / I / nervous / yesterday?

   → _____

9. Where / the station?

   → _____

10. Where / Peter / from?

    → _____

11. Why / they / in the kitchen / last night?

    → _____

12. What / those flowers?

    → _____

A Read each sentence. First write *yes/no* questions with the words in parentheses. Then complete the short answers.

1. I was sick yesterday. (he)   *Was he sick yesterday?*   No, *No, he wasn't* .

2. You were at the museum. (Bob)   _____   Yes, _____ .

3. We were nervous. (they)   _____   No, _____ .

4. Lisa was tired all the time. (you)   _____   No, _____ .

5. James is at home now. (Susan)   _____   Yes, _____ .

6. They are in Toronto. (Jane)   _____   No, _____ .

7. He was with the doctor. (the children)

_____   Yes, _____ .

B Read each sentence. Then write *wh-* questions with the words in parentheses.

1. I was angry yesterday. (why)   →   *Why was I angry yesterday?*

2. The girls were in the park. (when)   →   _____

3. Cindy was in the hospital. (why)   →   _____

C Make questions for each answer using *who*, *what*, or *where*.

1.

Q: *Who is she?*
A: She is my mother.

2.

Q: _____
A: Your laptop is on the desk.

3.

Q: _____
A: She is a police officer.

4.

Q: _____
A: The boy is my brother.

5.

Q: _____
A: He is my English teacher.

6.

Q: _____
A: She is in the kitchen.

D Write questions as in the example.

1. I saw a movie.	1. (good) _____ Was it good? _____
2. I met a famous actor.	2. (friendly) _____
3. I took an English exam.	3. (difficult) _____
4. I bought some books.	4. (expensive) _____
5. I went to a concert.	5. (interesting) _____

E Look at the pictures and write questions and answers as in the example.

1.
Alice is a teacher.

Q: Is she old? _____

A: No, she isn't. She is young. _____

old → No / young

2.
Kevin and Kristen are firefighters.

Q: _____

A: _____

at home now → No / at work

F Answer these questions about yourself.

1. What is your name?

_____

2. What was your grandfather?

_____

3. When is Christmas?

_____

4. When is your birthday?

_____

5. What is your favorite subject?

_____

6. What is your favorite sport?

_____

A Look at the example and practice with a partner. Use the words below or invent your own. (Repeat 3 times.)

1.

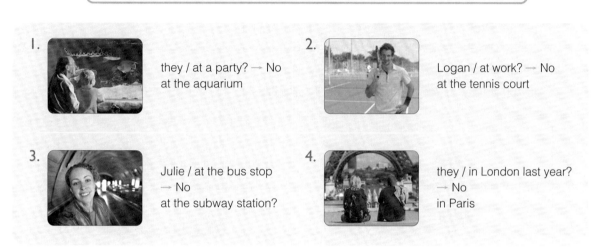

Were they at a party?   No, they weren't.

Where were they?   They were at the aquarium.

1. they / at a party? → No
at the aquarium

2. Logan / at work? → No
at the tennis court

3. Julie / at the bus stop
→ No
at the subway station?

4. they / in London last year?
→ No
in Paris

B Talk in pairs. Ask and answer personal questions (name, age, nationality, favorite sport/subject, etc.) and then write some sentences about your partner.

My partner is _____

_____

_____

_____

_____

_____

Hello, I'm Ryan. What's your name?

I'm Zack. Where are you from?

C Your partner chooses a job from the box. You ask questions to find out what he/she is. (E.g. Your partner chooses "soccer player".)

police officer	doctor	nurse
teacher	postman	singer
cook	porter	painter
waiter/waitress	soccer player	

Are you a doctor?
Are you a soccer player?

No, I'm not.
Yes, I am.

Unit 21 Questions: Action Verbs

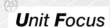

Unit Focus
▶ *Yes/No* Questions
▶ Information Questions with Action Verbs
▶ Questions with *Who* and *What* as the *Subject*

Yes/No Questions: Present, Past

- 일반 동사(Action Verbs)를 이용한 의문문을 만들 때에는 do, does 또는 did를 문장 맨 앞으로 보내고 물음표를 써 주기만 하면 돼요.

- 의문문에 대한 대답은 do/does/did를 이용하여 짧게 대답해요.

Present	Past
Q: **Do** you clean your room every day? A: Yes, I **do**. Q: **Do** you like K-pop music? A: No, I **don't**.	Q: **Did** Henry have lunch? A: Yes, he **did**. Q: **Did** he live in London last year? A: No, he **didn't**. He lived in New York.

Subject		Questions	Answers	
현재	I/you/we/they	Do you...?	Yes, I do.	No, I don't.
	he/she/it 등 3인칭 단수	Does he...?	Yes, he does.	No, he doesn't.
과거	모든 주어	Did she...?	Yes, she did.	No, she didn't.

Ⓐ **Make questions and complete the short answers.**

1. Brian has an art lesson on Monday.
   → Q: *Does Brian have an art lesson on Monday?*   A: Yes, *he does*.

2. It rained a lot last summer in Seoul.
   → Q: _____   A: Yes, _____.

3. Sunny and Tom bought new T-shirts.
   → Q: _____   A: No, _____.

126 Unit 21

Information Questions with Action Verbs

- 의문사가 있는 의문문의 어순은 '의문사 + do/does/did + 주어 + 동사 원형…?'으로 써요. 의문사를 이용해 궁금한 것을 자세히 물어보기 때문에 yes나 no로 대답할 수 없어요.

- 궁금한 것이 사람일 땐 who, 사물일 땐 what, 장소는 where, 시간이나 날짜는 when, 원인은 why, 방법이나 상태를 물을 땐 how를 써요.

Q: **What** do you want?

A: I want the MP3 player.

Q: **When** does Sora get up?

A: She gets up at 7 o'clock.

Q: **Where** did you go after school?

A: I went to the bookstore.

Who 누가 / What 무엇이, 무엇을		
When 언제 / Why 왜	do/does/did	주어 + 동사 원형…?
Where 어디서 / How 어떻게		

A Look at the pictures and circle the correct words for each answer.

1.

Q: (What /(Where)) (did /(does)) she work?

A: She works in a hospital.

2.

Q: (Who / What) (does / did) William do last weekend?

A: He played soccer on Sunday.

3.

Q: (Why / How) (does / do) you like that movie?

A: I love the actress.

4.

Q: (Why / When) (Bob visited / did Bob visit) his grandparents?

A: He visited them last weekend.

Questions with *Who* and *What* as the Subject

- 의문사(who, what) 자체가 주어가 되는 경우에는 조동사 역할을 하는 do, does, did를 함께 쓰지 않고 '의문사 + 동사 …?'의 어순으로 의문문을 만들어요.

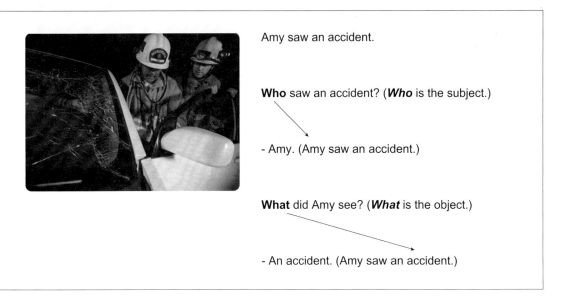

Amy saw an accident.

Who saw an accident? (**Who** is the subject.)

- Amy. (Amy saw an accident.)

What did Amy see? (**What** is the object.)

- An accident. (Amy saw an accident.)

WH- Word as Subject	Present/Past Tense Verb
Who	rang you?
What	Will happen next?

A Write questions with *who* or *what* (subject or object), as in the examples.

1. Someone smoked here. → *Who smoked here?*

2. I dropped something! → *What did you/I drop?*

3. Mary saw someone. → _____

4. I spoke to someone on the phone. → _____

5. Someone broke the vase. → _____

6. Something fell off the shelf. → _____

7. Someone took my phone. → _____

A Write *wh-* questions about the underlined words. Use *who*, *where*, *when*, or *why*.

1. Q: Where do your children go to school?

   A: My children go to school at <u>Seoul Elementary school</u>.

2. Q: _____

   A: They live on <u>40th street in Redmond</u>.

3. Q: _____

   A: Class begins at <u>8:00</u>.

4. Q: _____

   A: I bought a new bicycle <u>because I wanted to</u>.

5. Q: _____

   A: I met <u>Karen</u> yesterday.

B Look at Peter's agenda for yesterday. Make questions and write the correct answers.

- 8:00 walk the dog ( )
- 9:00 play golf with Tom (X)
- 11:00 water the flowers (✓)
- 12:00 cook lunch (X)
- 2:00 visit grandma (✓)
- 4:00 watch a DVD (✓)

1. Q: Did Peter walk the dog yesterday?   A: Yes, he did.

2. Q: _____   A: _____

3. Q: _____   A: _____

4. Q: _____   A: _____

5. Q: _____   A: _____

6. Q: _____   A: _____

C Make questions for the underlined words. Use *who* or *what*.

1. <u>Steve</u> broke that window. → *Who broke that window?*

2. Steve broke <u>that window</u>. → _____

3. I visited <u>my grandmother</u> on Sunday. → _____

4. <u>They</u> went to London last summer. → _____

5. My friend did <u>his homework</u> yesterday. → _____

6. <u>Nancy</u> lived in this house. → _____

7. Lisa saw <u>Bob</u>. → _____

8. The teacher looked at <u>the board</u>. → _____

9. <u>The teacher</u> looked at the board. → _____

D Answer these questions about yourself.

1. When do you get up? → *I get up at 7:00.*

2. What do you eat for breakfast? → _____

3. Who do you live with? → _____

4. When does school start? → _____

5. Does your school have good classes? → _____

6. What do you do on weekends? → _____

7. Do you have free time on weekends? → _____

8. When do you do your homework? → _____

9. Where do you go to school? → _____

10. Why do you go to school? → _____

A Look at the example and practice with a partner. Use the words below or invent your own. (Repeat 3 times.)

1.

Kathy went somewhere yesterday.

No, she didn't.

She went to the zoo.

Did she go to the theater?

Where did she go?

1. Kathy / go / somewhere / yesterday
the theater?
→ No / to the zoo

2. John / meet / someone / yesterday
his boss?
→ No / his girlfriend

3. Father / repair / something / yesterday
the car?
→ No / the computer

4. Ava / buy / something / yesterday
a new dress?
→ No / a new T-shirt

5. Emily / talk to / someone / yesterday
Scott?
→ No / Jason

B Work with a partner. Ask your partner questions with *When did you first/last...?*. Use the phrases below.

ride a bicycle

play a computer game

use a computer

stay at a friend's house

go on vacation

go to a costume party

go to a party

have a smartphone

When did you first ride a bicycle?

When I was seven years old.

Your turn to ask!

You are my
Grammar & Speaking

1
Workbook

Answer Key

Unit 1
p. 6

Simple Present of *Be*

Learn & Practice 1

A 1. is; He's 2. is; It's 3. are; You're 4. are; They're
   5. is; She's 6. am; I'm

Learn & Practice 2

A 1. isn't; is 2. am not; am 3. isn't; is 4. aren't; are
   5. aren't; are

Learn & Practice 3

A 1. Q: Is she a pianist? A: she isn't
   2. Q: Is it a fork? A: it is
   3. Q: Is the sun a ball of fire? A: it is
   4. Q: Are they vegetables? A: they aren't
   5. Q: Are you English teachers? A: we aren't

Learn & Practice 4

A 1. There is 2. There are 3. There is 4. There is
   5. There are 6. There are

B 1. A: Is B: isn't
   2. A: Is B: is
   3. A: Are B: aren't

Super Writing

A 1. Are there → No there aren't. There are six
      students in the classroom.
   2. Is there → Yes, there is.
   3. Are there → No, there aren't. There is one woman
      in the restaurant.
   4. Is there → No, there isn't. There is a fast food
      restaurant.

B 1. Q: Is she a nurse?
      A: No, she isn't.
   2. Q: Are you tired?
      A: No, I'm not.
   3. Q: Are the students in this class smart?
      A: Yes they are.

C 1. Is she 2. she is 3. she isn't 4. Is she 5. Is she
   6. she is 7. Is she 8. she is

D 1. David is from the USA. He is an actor. He is 44
      years old.

2. Yeonsu is from Korea. He is a cook. He is 32 years
   old.
3. Charlie and Harry are from England. They are
   police officers. Charlie is 36 years old and Harry is
   48 years old.

Unit 2
p. 12

Simple Present 1

Learn & Practice 1

A 1. reads 2. brushes 3. watches 4. swims 5. play
   6. takes place

Learn & Practice 2

A 1. float → floats 2. go → goes 3. have → has
   4. study → studies 5. brush → brushes
   6. try → tries 7. worry → worries 8. cost → costs

Learn & Practice 3

A 1. She doesn't like Japanese.
   2. I don't ride my bike in the park.
   3. My parents don't go to the movie theater on
      Sundays.
   4. Ava doesn't watch horro films.
   5. Karen doesn't have breakfast with her family.

Super Writing

A 1. A penguin doesn't live in Africa.
   2. Plants need water to grow.
   3. Rice doesn't grow on trees.
   4. A chicken doesn't give milk.

B 1. Julie Darcy is a very famous music star. She sings,
      she plays the drums, and she's a great dancer, too.
      Julie is an amazing drummer and she's only 10 years
      old! In her free time she likes going out with her
      friends, but she doesn't have much free time. Every
      day she goes to school, and then she has after-
      school activities.

C 1. She's a very famous music star.
   2. (She plays) The drums.
   3. She likes going out with her friends.

D 1. doesn't snow 2. doesn't speak
   3. don't remember 4. doesn't want 5. doesn't like

E **1.** doesn't drink coffee. She drinks milk.

2. doesn't do exercise. She does her homework every day.

3. doesn't ride his skateboard. He rides his bicycle.

4. doesn't watch TV on Thursdays. He watches DVDs on Thursdays.

Unit 3

p. 18

Simple Present 2

Learn & Practice 1

A **1.** Do **2.** Does **3.** Does **4.** Do **5.** Does **6.** Do

B **1.** Does Tom drink milk every day? - c

2. Does Ann teach French? - a

3. Do Bob and Kevin play baseball? - b

Learn & Practice 2

A **1.** does; come **2.** does; live **3.** do; go **4.** do; go

5. do; want

B **1.** Where does your brother sleep?

2. Where do you play soccer?

3. Where does Tom eat lunch every day?

4. Where does Steve wait for the bus?

Learn & Practice 3

A **1.** What does; d **2.** What does; e **3.** What does; b

4. What do; a **5.** What does; c

Super Writing

A **1.** Q: Does A: does **2.** Q: Do A: don't

3. Q: Do A: do **4.** Q: Does A: does

5. Q: Does A: does

B **1.** Does Janet eat lunch at the cafeteria every day?

2. Where does Janet eat lunch every day?

3. Does Richard eat dinner at a restaurant every day?

4. Where does Richard eat dinner every day?

5. Does Hyemi work at a broadcasting station?

6. Where does Hyemi work?

7. Do firefighters work at a fire station?

8. Where do firefighters work?

C **1.** Q: Does the shop close at 8:00 p.m. on Saturday?

A: No, the shop doesn't close at 8:00 p.m. on Saturday. It closes at 9:00 p.m.

2. Q: Does Ms. Lane like ice cream?

A: No, Ms. Lane doesn't like ice cream. She likes banana cake.

3. Q: Does Tom's father work on the weekend?

A: No, Tom's father doesn't work on the weekend. He plays sports.

4. Q: Does Sandy clean the house on Friday?

A: No, Sandy doesn't clean the house on Friday. She washes the car.

D **1.** What does Ava do in the afternoon? She watches TV.

2. What does Jason do on Sundays? He plays computer games.

Unit 4

p. 24

Present Progressive 1

Learn & Practice 1

A **1.** She is drinking water.

2. Those girls are taking a picture.

3. Nancy is riding her bicycle.

Learn & Practice 2

A

Add -*ing*	Drop -e and add -*ing*	Double the consonant, add -*ing*
playing	saving	getting
repairing	moving	putting
wearing	hoping	stopping
washing	dancing	swimming
reading	smiling	cutting

Learn & Practice 3

A **1.** (P) Nancy is sleeping. (N) Nancy isn't sleeping.

2. (P) Tom is drinking milk.

(N) Tom isn't drinking milk.

3. (P) They are playing badminton.

(N) They aren't playing badminton.

B **1.** isn't playing **2.** isn't riding **3.** isn't buying

Super Writing

A **1.** No, he isn't sleeping. He is playing.

2. No, she isn't eating. She is drinking water.

135

3. No, she isn't working. She is eating a hamburger.

4. No, he isn't sitting under a tree. He is climbing a tree.

5. No, they aren't taking a picture. They are walking to school.

6. No, he isn't talking on the phone. He is taking a shower.

B 1. → They aren't playing basketball.

    → They are playing soccer.

2. → She isn't painting a picture.

    → She is listening to music.

3. → They aren't eating pizza.

    → They are reading a book.

C 1. The woman is speaking on her phone.

2. The woman (= She) is holding her credit card.

3. The woman (= She) is looking at her credit card.

4. The woman (= She) is wearing a white dress.

5. The man is working on his laptop.

6. The man (= He) is wearing a striped shirt.

7. The man (= He) is wearing blue jeans.

8. The man and woman (= They) are sitting on a chair.

Unit 5
Present Progressive 2
p. 30

Learn & Practice 1

A 1. Is she working hard? | she isn't

2. Are they writing a composition? | they are

3. Is he cutting the cake? | he isn't

Learn & Practice 2

A 1. future 2. present 3. future 4. present

5. present 6. future 7. future

Learn & Practice 3

A 1. Who; b 2. What; c 3. What; a 4. Who; d

Super Writing

A 1. Q: Are they studying English at a language school?

    A: No, they aren't. They are taking a picture.

2. Q: Are they waiting for the train?

    A: No, they aren't. They are studying in the library.

3. Q: Is Jane listening to music?

    A: No, she isn't. She is taking the subway.

B 1. Q: Who is waiting for the train?

2. A: They are having dinner.

3. Q: Who is climbing the tree?

4. A: They are painting the house.

5. Q: Who is taking off the clothes?

6. A: They are taking taekwondo lessons.

C A: What are you doing on Monday night?

B: I'm going to the movie theater.

A: Who are you going with?

B: I'm going with Cindy.

A: What time are you meeting her?

B: At 7 o'clock.

A: And what about on Wednesday? Are you going out?

B: Yes I am. I'm going to a family restaurant.

A: Are you staying at home on Friday?

B: No, I am meeting Peter at the airport.

A: What time is he arriving?

B: At 8:00.

A: Are you staying at home on Saturday?

B: No, we are visiting the museum.

D Dad: Hi, Kevin. How are you doing?

Kevin: Fine. How about you?

Dad: Good. How's everyone?

Kevin: They're doing fine.

Dad: What are you doing, Kevin?

Kevin: I'm watching TV.

Dad: What is Jennifer doing?

Kevin: Jennifer (= She) is reading a book.

Dad: What is Bob doing?

Kevin: Bob (= He) is listening to music.

Dad: What is grandfather doing?

Kevin: Grandfather (= He) is surfing the Internet.

Unit 6
Nouns, Articles
p. 36

Learn & Practice 1

A

people	animals	places	things
girl	lion	theater	book
brother	elephant	restaurant	computer
doctor	kangaroo	museum	desk

B 1. Kim and Stephanie wore masks on Halloween.

2. The tourists visited Rome and saw the Colosseum.

Learn & Practice 2

A 1. a 2. An 3. an 4. a 5. a; an 6. an

Learn & Practice 3

A 1. leaves 2. ladies 3. schools 4. forests 5. buses
6. bookcases 7. families 8. bushes 9. benches

Learn & Practice 4

A 1. children 2. fish 3. feet 4. geese 5. women
6. mice

Super Writing

A 1. babies 2. butterflies 3. cities 4. countries
5. dictionaries 6. discoveries 7. ladies 8. libraries
9. parties

B 1. child; children; children; children; children; one child
2. mice; mice; mice; mice; one mouse
3. women; women; women; women; one woman
4. teeth; teeth; teeth; teeth; one tooth

C 1. is French. She is a fashion model. She has got black
hair and brown eyes. She can dance and swim.
2. is Swedish. She is an architect. She has got blond
hair and blue eyes. She can play tennis and sing.
3. is American. He is an electrician. He has got black
hair and grey eyes. He can drive and play baseball.

D 1. He is a taxi driver.
2. He is an auto mechanic.
3. She is a firefighter.
4. He is an engineer.

Unit 7

Pronouns, Demonstratives

p. 42

Learn & Practice 1

A 1. they 2. we 3. you 4. it 5. they 6. they 7. it
8. she

B 1. It 2. He 3. They 4. It

Learn & Practice 2

A 1. him 2. it 3. them 4. me 5. her

B 1. her 2. him 3. it 4. us 5. them

Learn & Practice 3

A 1. These 2. Those 3. it 4. Those are
5. these; They

Super Writing

A 1. She is our English teacher.
2. She uses it to teach grammar.
3. We study English at the same school.
4. She teaches us grammar.
5. The students like her.
6. They ask her questions.
7. She answers them.
8. She always asks questions.

B 1. It leaves at 9:00.
2. He has moved to Seattle.
3. They are on the table.
4. I like them.
5. She is traveling to France.
6. No, it isn't. It is difficult.

C 1. That is a mountain.
2. These are horses.
3. Those are trees.
4. This is a cheetah.
5. Those are ducks.
6. This is a crocodile.

D 1. Are those; No, they aren't. They are watermelons.
2. Is this; No, it isn't. It is a wolf.
3. Are these; No, they aren't. They are ostriches.

Unit 8

Possessives

p. 48

Learn & Practice 1

A 1. my handkerchief 2. her scarf 3. their car

Learn & Practice 2

A 1. Joe's dog
2. Ann's house
3. the girls' book
4. the children's money
5. the man's hat

Learn & Practice 3

A 1. mine 2. hers 3. His 4. Ours 5. yours

Learn & Practice 4

A 1. Q: is A: Sandra's
2. Q: are A: his
3. Q: is A: Tom's

137

4. Q: are   A: our

5. Q: is   A: hers

6. Q: are   A: their

Super Writing

A **1.** Q: Whose skirt   A: It's my skirt. It's mine.

2. Q: Whose T-shirt   A: It's your T-shirt. It's yours.

3. Q: Whose boots   A: They're her boots. They're hers.

4. Q: Whose keys   A: They're his keys. They're his.

5. Q: Whose ball   A: It's their ball. It's thiers.

B **1.** Yes, it is. It is his bike.

2. Yes, it is. It is his truck.

3. Yes, it is. It is her blackboard.

4. Yes, it is. It is their dog.

5. Yes, it is. It is her umbrella.

C **1.** Q: Whose computer is that?

A: It's the children's.

2. Q: Whose umbrella is that?

A: It's Paul's.

3. Q: Whose ice skates are those?

A: They're Alice's.

4. Q: Whose soccer ball is that?

A: It's the girls'.

D **1.** William's favorite food is spaghetti. His favorite sport is golf. His favorite singer is Rihanna. His favorite movie star is Megan Fox.

2. Cindy's favorite food is chicken. Her favorite sport is swimming. Her favorite singer is Justin Timberlake. Her favorite movie star is Johnny Depp.

3. Bob and Jane's favorite food is fish and chips. Their favorite sport is soccer. Their favorite singer is Elton John. Their favorite movie star is Angelina Jolie.

Unit 9
Count/Noncount Nouns, Quantity Questions p. 54

Learn & Practice 1

A

Count	Noncount
egg	ice cream
dress	homework
sandwich	salt

Learn & Practice 2

A **1.** tube   **2.** slices/pieces

Learn & Practice 3

A **1.** some   **2.** an   **3.** any

Learn & Practice 4

A **1.** How many   **2.** How much   **3.** How much

4. How much   **5.** How many   **6.** How many

B **1.** are → is   **2.** much → many   **3.** moneys → money

4. many → much

Super Writing

A **1.** How much coffee is there in the cup?

2. How much Coke is there in the bottle?

3. How many eggs are there in the fridge?

4. How much tea is there in the cup?

5. How many tomatoes are there in the bag?

6. How much soup is there in the bowl?

7. How much strawberry juice is there in the glass?

B **1.** Is there any milk on the table; there is some milk

2. Is there any bread; there is some bread

3. Are there any onions; there aren't any onions

4. Are there any apples; there are some apples

5. Is there any rice; there isn't any rice

6. Is there any orange juice; there is some orange juice

D **1.** Q: Is there any bread in the basket?

A: Yes, there is some bread.

2. Q: How many wine glasses are there on the picnic cloth?

A: There are three wine glasses.

3. Q: Is there any cheese on the table?

A: Yes, there is some cheese.

4. Q: How many bottles of milk are there on the table?

A: There is a bottle of milk.

5. Q: Are there any oranges in the fridge?

A: Yes, there are some oranges.

6. Q: How much juice is there in the fridge?

A: There is some juice. / There are three bottles of juice.

Unit 10
Will, Articles (Definite/Zero) p. 60

Learn & Practice 1

A **1.** go (Instant Decisions)

2. will carry (Instant Decisions)

3. be (Future Predictions)

4. will help (Instant Decisions)

B **1.** It will be warm tomorrow.

2. Olivia's party will be fun.

3. Bob won't watch the match.

4. William will study all weekend.

5. Laura won't do any work.

Learn & Practice 2

A **1.** Q: Will she make a sandwich?   A: she won't

2. Q: Will it be cold tomorrow?   A: it will

3. Q: Will he be a third grader next year?   A: he will

Learn & Practice 3

A **1.** × **2.** × **3.** the **4.** the **5.** × **6.** The **7.** a

8. ×; ×

Super Writing

A **1.** The sun **2.** the flute **3.** the guitar **4.** The sky

5. math

B **1.** Q: Will you be at home tomorrow night?

A: I won't

2. Q: Will Jane meet her family next Christmas?

A: she will

3. Q: Will Jason and Cindy be at the party?

A: they won't

4. Q: Will Jessica arrive in Seoul next week?

A: she will

C **1.** I will shut the window.

2. I will have (the) chicken(, please).

3. I will carry the/your bag (for you).

4. I will post it (= the letter) (for you).

D **1.** Q: Will I go to Seoul National University?

A: No, you won't. You'll go to Yonsei University.

2. Q: Will I become a movie star?

A: No, you won't. You'll become a teacher.

3. Q: Will I get married?

A: Yes, you will.

4. Q: Will my husband and I have two children?

A: No, you won't. You'll have five children.

5. Q: Will we live in Seoul?

A: No, you won't. You'll live in Busan.

E ×; a; a; a; an; a; The; the; ×; the

Unit 11
p. 66

Simple Past of *Be*

Learn & Practice 1

A **1.** was **2.** were **3.** were **4.** was **5.** was **6.** were

B **1.** was **2.** was **3.** is **4.** are **5.** were **6.** was

Learn & Practice 2

A **1.** she wasn't here

2. she wasn't busy

3. he wasn't at the library

4. they weren't at my house

5. you weren't in sports class

6. it wasn't cold

7. she wasn't my classmate

Learn & Practice 3

A **1.** Q: Was it rainy yesterday?

A: it was

2. : Was she at home yesterday?

A: she wasn't

3. Q: Was Tom tired last night?

A: he was

4. Q: Was the movie great?

A: it wasn't

5. Q: Were they in class yesterday?

A: they were

6. Q: Were Lisa and you at the park?

A: we weren't

Super Writing

A **1.** Q: Was Mozart a painter?

A: No, he wasn't. He was a musician.

2. Q: Was Van Gogh from Germany?

A: No, he wasn't. He was from Holland.

3. Q: Was Cleopatra American?

A: No, she wasn't. She was Egyptian.

4. Q: Was Alexander Graham Bell an architect?

A: No, he wasn't. He was an inventor.

B **1.** was; was; were; were; was; was; was; was - a

2. was; were; was; was; was; was; was - d

D **1.** Q: Were you at a restaurant last Saturday?

A: Yes, we were.

2. Q: Were you in Egypt last week?

A: Yes, I was. / Yes, we were.

139

3. Q: Were Nancy and Peter in the movie theater yesterday?

A: Yes, they were.

4. Q: Were they at the art gallery last Monday?

A: No, they weren't.

Unit 12
Simple Past 1
p. 72

Learn & Practice 1
A **1.** rained **2.** didn't walk **3.** asked **4.** didn't play
5. watched **6.** didn't stay

Learn & Practice 2
A **1.** Q: Did Elizabeth graduate last summer?

A: she did

2. Q: Did they invite six people?

A: they didn't

3. Q: Did the guests arrive on time?

A: they did

4. Q: Did the fire start in the oven?

A: it didn't

5. Q: Did the shop close ten minutes ago?

A: it did

6. Q: Did she walk to school yesterday?

A: she didn't

7. Q: Did he open the windows?

A: he did

Learn & Practice 3
A **1.** wanted **2.** walked **3.** loved **4.** tried **5.** stopped
6. dropped **7.** planned **8.** studied **9.** played
10. helped **11.** stayed **12.** lived
B **1.** Nancy called me.
2. Bob didn't clean his room.
3. Tiffany worked at a bakery.
4. She listened to the customers very carefully.
5. Sam didn't visit Paris.

Super Writing
A **1.** Yesterday I didn't ask the teacher a question.
2. The government didn't create two million jobs in the last few years.
3. Yesterday she didn't listen to music on the radio.
4. Other nations didn't invest their money in the

United States.
5. The country didn't face serious economic problems.
6. Kevin didn't stay home in the evening.
B **1.** No, she didn't. She listened to music.
2. No, they didn't. They played soccer.
3. No, she didn't. She walked on the beach.
4. No, they didn't. They stayed at home.
D **1.** Did Rachel wash her face?

A: No, she didn't. She washed her hands.

2. Q: Did Emma and Henry watch a movie on television?

A: No, they didn't. They visited their grandparents.

3. Q: Did Smith paint a picture two weeks ago?

A: No, he didn't. He painted a house.

4. Q: Did the children study for the chemistry test yesterday?

A: No, they didn't. They studied for the history test.

Unit 13
Simple Past 2
p. 78

Learn & Practice 1
A **1.** told **2.** was **3.** ran **4.** met **5.** read **6.** slept
7. flew **8.** ate **9.** made **10.** had **11.** drank
12. took
B **1.** I saw my grandparents last weekend.
2. They went to the mountains last summer.
3. Julie met William from school this afternoon.
4. She ate a lot last night.
5. We had a nice time with them on holiday.
6. Tom did exercise for half an hour yesterday.
C **1.** sat on the bench
2. did the laundry
3. took a bath
4. drank a lot of water

Learn & Practice 2
A **1.** What **2.** Why **3.** When **4.** Where **5.** Who
6. What

Super Writing
A **1.** No, I didn't. I ate lunch at the cafeteria.
2. No, he didn't. He went to the library last night.
3. No, she didn't. She had a cup of green tea this morning.

4. No, they didn't. They came to school by bus yesterday.

B 1. Where did you go last night?
2. When did Cindy arrive in Seoul?
3. What did Kevin eat for lunch?
4. Who did you see at the concert?
5. Why did Laura stay home last night?

C 1. She had a picnic.
2. She played beach volleyball.
3. She swam in the sea.
4. She saw a fireworks display.

E 1. What did you see?
2. Who did you see?
3. When did you see her?
4. How did she look?
5. Who discovered penicillin?
6. Why did you run?

2. They're sitting across from us.
3. It is in the rack above my head.
4. It is under his seat.
5. It is between our seats and the pretty ladies' seats.
6. It is under the dining table.

C 1. The sofa is below the pictures.
2. The wardrobe is next to the window.
3. The mirror is above the washbasin.
4. The television is on the table.
5. The stereo is on the table. / The stereo is next to the television.
6. The pictures are above the sofa.

D 1. The bank is next to the bookstore.
2. The fountain is in front of the theater.
3. The bookstore is across from the theater.
4. The bookstore is between the bank and the supermarket.
5. Paul's office is near the supermarket/bank.

Unit 14
Prepositions of Place
p. 84

Learn & Practice 1
A 1. On the wall.
2. At the airport.
3. Under the tree.
4. In the box.

Learn & Practice 2
A 1. behind   2. next to   3. between   4. behind
5. next to   6. between

Learn & Practice 3
A 1. Above the bed.
2. In front of the Eiffel Tower.
3. Across from the building.
4. Near the coast.

Super Writing
A 1. No, it isn't. It is in front of the chair.
2. It is on the bed.
3. It is on the floor.
4. No, it isn't. It is under the bed.
5. It is on the wall. / It is above the bed.
6. They are in the basket.

B 1. I'm sitting next to my friend Bob.

Unit 15
Prepositions of Time
p. 90

Learn & Practice 1
A 1. on   2. at   3. on   4. on   5. in   6. at

Learn & Practice 2
A 1. c   2. d   3. e   4. b   5. a
B 1. at   2. on   3. on   4. on   5. in   6. at
C 1. When does the supermarket open?
2. What time does the bank close?
3. When is your birthday?
4. When do you visit your grandmother?
5. When does your brother graduate from high school?

Super Writing
A 1. Tom and I went to a shopping mall on Saturday.
2. We have classes in the morning.
3. School starts at 8 o'clock in the morning.
4. I have my guitar lessons at 10:00 on Wednesdays.
B 1. on   2. at   3. In   4. On
C 1. On; at; in; at; At; on; at; in; at; at; at; at
D 1. Her favorite day is Saturday.
2. She gets up at 7:00 in the morning.
3. After lunch, she watches DVDs or listens to classical

music.

4. TRUE

5. She has dinner at 8:00 in the evening.

6. TRUE

E **1.** When / What time do you have dinner?

   2. When is Halloween?

   3. When / What time do you go to bed?

   4. What day is Halloween?

   5. When is Christmas?

   6. When / What time does the train leave?

Unit 16
p. 96

Adjectives

Learn & Practice 1

A **1.** She has beautiful eyes.

   2. That is a round table.

   3. Tom is a nice businessman.

   4. It is a yellow lemon.

Learn & Practice 2

A **1.** are small rooms

   2. is not a long story

   3. are happy children

   4. is a quiet village

   5. are heavy books

B **1.** noun   **2.** adjective   **3.** adjective   **4.** adjective

   5. noun

Learn & Practice 3

A **1.** The girl is pretty.

   2. The girls are happy.

   3. The monkeys are hungry.

   4. The ruler is long.

B **1.** Korean   **2.** Australian   **3.** Japanese   **4.** Brazilian

   5. German   **6.** Russian

Super Writing

A **1.** is a crowded bookstore

   2. is an expensive jewelry store

   3. is a noisy music store

   4. are kind salespeople

   5. are happy children

   6. is a clean restaurant

   7. is a beautiful waitress

8. is an old waiter

B **1.** Lisa isn't Egyptian. She is Italian.

   2. She is single. She isn't married.

   3. She isn't ugly. She is pretty.

   4. She isn't short. She is tall.

   5. She is slim. She isn't fat.

C **1.** He looks angry beause his dog chewed up his shoes.

   2. She seems happy because she got an A+ on the English test.

   3. She looks sad because she lost her dog.

   4. He seems tired because he ran a marathon.

D **1.** car key   **2.** rope bridge   **3.** walking shoes

   4. wedding dress

Unit 17
p. 102

Adverbs

Learn & Practice 1

A **1.** The boys walked quickly.

   2. It looks very nice.

   3. They arrived early.

   4. They started the race slowly.

   5. I'm really nervous.

   6. In April it often rains heavily.

B **1.** beautifully (How)

   2. outside (Where)

   3. late (When)

   4. here (Where)

Learn & Practice 2

A **1.** happily   **2.** quickly   **3.** easily   **4.** slowly   **5.** carefully

   6. hard   **7.** fast   **8.** well   **9.** safely   **10.** badly

   11. angrily   **12.** late

Learn & Practice 3

A **1.** Kelly is always on time.

   2. My mom sometimes cooks breakfast.

   3. Kelly always comes to work on time.

   4. We never eat hamburgers.

   5. He is often at work on Sundays.

B **1.** How often do

   2. How often does

   3. How often do

   4. How often does

5. How often does

6. How often do

Super Writing

A **1.** always takes the school bus

2. often goes to the zoo

3. sometimes go shopping on Sunday

4. never washes clothes by hand

B **1.** She is a very careful person.

2. Yes, she works hard.

3. She usually drives very carefully.

4. She sometimes takes a subway.

5. She drove badly yesterday evening.

6. No, but she almost had an accident.

C **1.** carefully **2.** beautifully **3.** fluently **4.** well

5. hard **6.** sadly

D **1.** Jason usually does his homework at 6:00 in the evening.

2. He usually has dinner at 7:00 in the evening.

3. He usually watches TV at 8:00 in the evening.

4. He usually goes to bed at 9:00 in the evening.

Unit 18

p. 108

Helping Verbs

Learn & Practice 1

A **1.** can jump; can't climb

2. can't drive; can ride

3. can walk; can't run

4. can sleep; can't live

B **1.** Q: Can Yuri speak English? A: she can

2. Q: Could they go on a picnic? A: they couldn't

3. Q: Can Tom finish his homework? A: he can't

4. Q: Could Sunny and Bob dance? A: they could

Learn & Practice 2

A **1.** It may rain tomorrow.

2. She will go to the interview.

3. He may go to the duty-free shop.

4. I will show you the family photos.

5. The sun will rise tomorrow morning.

6. This street may be dangerous at night.

Learn & Practice 3

A **1.** May **2.** Can **3.** May

B **1.** ability **2.** possibility **3.** permission **4.** possibility

5. permission **6.** ability

Super Writing

A **1.** Ava can drive a car now. When she was younger, she could only ride a bicycle.

2. Susan can cook spaghetti now. When she was younger, she could only make sandwiches.

3. Tom can read a newspaper now. When he was younger, he could only draw pictures.

4. John can play water polo now. When he was younger, he could only play basketball.

C **1.** she may have an accident

2. he may sell his laptop

3. she may become a fashion designer

4. they may go to the stadium

D **1.** May I use your phone, please?

2. Can I borrow your calculator, please?

3. May I borrow your dictionary, please?

4. Can I bring you some comic books to read?

5. May I have the check, please?

6. Can I use the telephone, please?

Unit 19

p. 114

Imperatives, Let's

Learn & Practice 1

A **1.** Please don't lose weight.

2. Please don't wait for me.

3. Don't read this magazine tonight.

4. Don't go out for dinner, please.

5. Don't wash your hands.

B **1.** Turn **2.** Don't pick **3.** Cross **4.** Write

5. Don't park **6.** Do not enter **7.** don't smoke

8. Don't hunt **9.** Don't use

Learn & Practice 2

A **1.** Let's **2.** Let's **3.** Let's **4.** Let's not **5.** Let's

B **1.** c; Let's **2.** d; Don't **3.** f; Let's **4.** a; Let's

5. b; Don't **6.** e; Don't

Super Writing

A **1.** Turn off **2.** Don't eat **3.** Don't smoke

4. Don't run **5.** Turn down **6.** Take

B **1.** Let's not make dinner.

2. Let's play basketball.

3. Let's not swim here.

4. Let's go to see a doctor.

C **1.** Don't eat food at night.

  2. Exercise/Jog every day. OR Exercise/Jog in the morning.

  3. Don't eat hamburgers.

  4. Eat a lot of vegetables.

D **1.** Let's go for a picnic.

  2. Let's go to Linda's house-warming party.

  3. Let's go swimming.

  4. Let's watch TV.

  5. Let's have lunch at that French restaurant.

E **1.** No, don't sleep late.

  2. No, let's not take a taxi.

  3. No, let's not order pizza.

  4. No, don't wait for me.

  5. No, don't paint the door.

  6. No, don't call me tonight.

  7. No, let's not go to school now.

  8. No, don't close the window.

Unit 20
Questions: the Verb *Be*
p. 120

Learn & Practice 1
A **1.** Were you tired last night?

  2. Is Sunny at home?

  3. Was he a teacher ten years ago?

B **1.** Is; it is **2.** Am; you aren't **3.** Was; she was

  4. Were; they weren't **5.** Is; he is

Learn & Practice 2
A **1.** Where is John?

  2. Where was John yesterday?

  3. Why are they hungry?

  4. How is the food?

  5. When is the concert?

  6. Why were you late yesterday?

  7. How was she last night?

  8. Why was I nervous yesterday?

  9. Where is the station?

  10. Where is Peter from?

  11. Why were they in the kitchen last night?

  12. What are those flowers?

Super Writing

A **1.** Q: Was he sick yesterday?   A: he wasn't

  2. Q: Was Bob at the museum?   A: he was

  3. Q: Were they nervous?   A: they weren't

  4. Q: Were you tired all the time?   A: I wasn't / we weren't

  5. Q: Is Susan at home now?   A: she is

  6. Q: Is Jane in Toronto?   A: she isn't

  7. Q: Were the children with the doctor?
     A: they were

B **1.** Why was I angry yesterday?

  2. When were the girls in the park?

  3. Why was Cindy in the hospital?

C **1.** Who is she?

  2. Where is my laptop?

  3. What is she?

  4. Who is the boy?

  5. Who is he?

  6. Where is she?

D **1.** Was it good?

  2. Was he friendly?

  3. Was it difficult?

  4. Were they expensive?

  5. Was it intersting?

E **1.** Q: Is she old?
     A: No, she isn't. She is young.

  2. Q: Are they at home now?
     A: No, they aren't. They are at work.

Unit 21
Questions: Action Verbs
p. 126

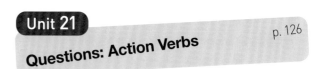

Learn & Practice 1
A **1.** Q: Does Brian have an art lesson on Monday?
     A: he does

  2. Q: Did it rain a lot last summer in Seoul?   A: it did

  3. Q: Did Sunny and Tom buy new T-shirts?
     A: they didn't

Learn & Practice 2
A **1.** Where does **2.** What did **3.** Why do

  4. When did Bob visit

Learn & Practice 3

A 1. Who smoked here?

   2. What did you/I drop?

   3. Who did Mary/she see?

   4. Who did you speak to on the phone?

   5. Who broke the vase?

   6. What fell off the shelf?

   7. Who took my/your phone?

Super Writing

A 1. Where do your children go to school?

   2. Where do they live?

   3. When does class begin?

   4. Why did you buy a new bicycle?

   5. Who did you meet yesterday?

B 1. Q: Did peter walk the dog yesterday?

     A: Yes, he did.

   2. Q: Did Peter play golf with Tom yesterday?

     A: No, he didn't.

   3. Q: Did Peter water the flowers yesterday?

     A: Yes, he did.

   4. Q: Did Peter cook lunch?

     A: No, he didn't.

   5. Q: Did Peter visit his grandma yesterday?

     A: Yes, he did.

   6. Q: Did Peter watch a DVD yesterday?

     A: Yes, he did.

C 1. Who broke that window?

   2. What did Steve break?

   3. Who did you visit on Sunday?

   4. Who went to London last summer?

   5. What did your friend do yesterday?

   6. Who lived in this house?

   7. Who did Lisa see?

   8. What did the teacher look at?

   9. Who looked at the board?

146